HEA
2000 Y
P H I L I

SUTTON PUBLISHING LIM

D1344139

Sutton Publishing Limited
Phoenix Mill · Thrupp · Stroud
Gloucestershire · GL5 2BU

First published in 1990 as *The History of
Heathrow*

Reprinted in 2001

Copyright © Philip Sherwood, 1999

British Library Cataloguing in Publication Data
A catalogue record for this book is available from the
British Library.

ISBN 0-7509-2132-3

Typeset in 10/11 Bembo.
Typesetting and origination by
Sutton Publishing Limited.
Printed in Great Britain by
J.H. Haynes & Co. Ltd, Sparkford.

Philip Sherwood has long family connections with the Heathrow area, where he was born and still lives. Locally he attended Sipson and Heathrow Elementary School and Bishopshalt Grammar School, went on to obtain a degree in Chemistry from the University of London and later became a Fellow of the Royal Society of Chemistry. As a Principal Scientific Officer in the Scientific Civil Service he has worked for the Transport (formerly Road) Research Laboratory and the Royal Commission on Environmental Pollution. Since leaving full-time employment he has written several books both on his work experience and on local history and is well known as a lecturer in these fields. He is an active member of several amenity and environmental organisations, the Treasurer of the Hayes and Harlington Local History Society and Chairman of the local branch of the Council for the Protection of Rural England.

Title page photograph: Perry Oaks Farm, 1935. Perry Oaks is now the name of a well-known sludge works and the possible site of a fifth terminal for Heathrow Airport. Long before this, the fine old Elizabethan red-bricked Perry Oaks Farm had been almost the only building in the Perry Oaks area of Heathrow. It was demolished in 1949 in the second phase of the development of the airport.

CONTENTS

Heathrow under construction, 1945. Test pilot, Bill Humble, in a Tempest II from Langley airfield, flying over Heathrow in 1945. The Perry Oaks sludge works can be seen in the right foreground under the wing of the aircraft. Reproduced, by permission, from the Michael Stroud photo collection.

FOREWORD

There are many accounts of Heathrow, mostly written by civil aviation enthusiasts. These, together with the self-congratulatory propaganda of BAA and British Airways, mean that the civil aviation aspect of Heathrow is well covered and yet another book on this subject would be superfluous. Less well known is the long history of the Heathrow area which is quite separate from the airport. Nor is the effect that the growth of the airport has had on the once pleasant and peaceful countryside of West Middlesex, which has been destroyed in less than fifty years, ever considered. The book therefore concentrates on these aspects. The change from a relatively prosperous, largely agricultural area, to the world's busiest international airport is often referred to as progress – a word which the dictionary defines as 'an advance to something better or later in development'. Anybody who can remember what the Heathrow area was like before the advent of the airport will surely agree that progress is hardly the appropriate word.

The development of the airport has totally changed the social structure of the communities living around it. Many of these now depend on the airport for their economic well-being and resent any criticism of it. However, as relative newcomers, they should accept that there are those who are even more resentful of the manner in which the airport came about. They are, in any case, outnumbered by those who live within ear-shot of Heathrow who derive no benefit from it but are reminded every minute of the day of its presence. Ever since the airport was established the rights of people have been subordinated to the interests of civil aviation to the point where one could say of Heathrow, as Goldsmith wrote in his poem 'The Deserted Village': 'Ill fares the land to hast'ning ills a prey, where wealth accumulates and men decay.'

The fact that Heathrow plays a vital role in the national economy cannot be questioned, but the major British airport would be bound to play such a role wherever it was situated. The argument against Heathrow as the site for the major airport is that it was singularly ill chosen and the development should not have taken place by what many would regard as fraud. The claim has always been made that Heathrow was developed as a result of an urgent wartime need for the RAF to have a bomber base in the London area. Research among the Air Ministry files in the Public Record Office shows that there was never such a need and the airfield was developed from the start as a civil airport for London. The War Cabinet was deceived into giving approval for the development, even though it meant diverting resources away from the war effort when preparations were being made for the Normandy landings. The Defence of the Realm Act 1939 was used by the Air Ministry to requisition the land and to circumvent the public inquiry that would otherwise have had to be held. The book describes the results of the examination of the files, which show the true story behind the development.

Elated with its success in establishing the airport in this way during the latter part of the Second World War, the civil aviation lobby has continued ever since to seek to expand the airport boundaries. The attempt to build a fifth terminal is only the latest of these plans. Each proposed expansion is claimed at the time to be the last but, once permission is given, it inevitably leads to further demands. The fourth terminal, which BAA claimed to be its last-ever demand, was followed within three years of its opening by an application to build a fifth terminal! No doubt, if this were to be permitted, it would inevitably be followed by a demand for additional runway capacity, which in turn would be followed by proposals for a sixth terminal.

The debate over Terminal 5 is set to be the landmark planning issue of the turn of the century and the subject of the longest Inquiry since those into nuclear power-station extensions some fifteen years ago. These earlier inquiries were lost by the opposition groups, not because they were wrong, but because the nuclear industry presented arguments that have subsequently been shown to be grossly misleading and the true costs of producing nuclear energy were under-estimated. The aviation industry may similarly succeed in its aims but it will have a much more difficult task because much of what it proposes runs counter to recent changes in attitudes to environmental degradation. If it does succeed, it will be a pyrrhic victory because in the long term what is being proposed is simply unsustainable.

The philosophy of 'predict and provide' has belatedly been abandoned in road-building as it has become increasingly apparent that the predictions are largely self-fulfilling – traffic grows to fill the space available. The same is equally true of air transport and it is to be hoped that it will eventually be realised that we cannot simply go on extrapolating ever-rising forecasts of growth in air traffic indefinitely into the future without unacceptable environmental consequences. In the words of Michael Heseltine, when Secretary of State for the Environment (1992), 'We have now reached the point where we cannot always respond to demands for either development or transport infrastructure simply because those demands exist.'

As a society we will need to pay a higher price for air travel to offset the unacceptable disturbance that is caused by the civil aviation industry. Until such time is reached it will never prove possible to write a history of Heathrow that will remain up-to-date for very long.

P.T. Sherwood
Harlington, 1999

CHAPTER ONE

PRE-AIRPORT MAPS & AERIAL VIEWS

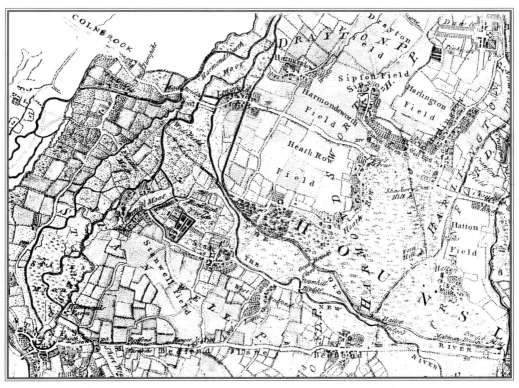

Rocque's Map of Middlesex, 1754. The earliest known large-scale (2 miles to the inch) map of the area. The Bath Road runs east–west across the middle of the map with Harmondsworth, Sipson and Harlington to its north and Heathrow to the south. Rocque gives the name as Heath Row but nearly all other sources of information, before and since, give it as one word. Heathrow is shown as being on the edge of Hounslow Heath, forming part of the common land of Harmondsworth Parish, and to the west of Heathrow Road is Heathrow Field, one of the pre-Inclosure open arable fields of Harmondsworth Parish. Comparison of Rocque's map with the Harmondsworth Inclosure map shows that, apart from the Bath Road and Heathrow Road, most of the roads in the area were re-aligned at the time of the Inclosure. In the otherwise flat landscape, Rocque defines two areas close to the Harmondsworth/ Harlington parish boundary as Shasbury Hill and Fern Hill (see page 14).

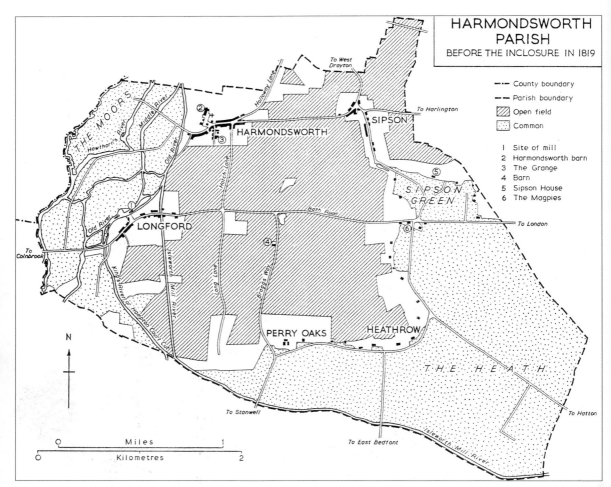

Harmondsworth Parish before Inclosure. This map combines the information in Rocque's map (page 7) and the Harmondsworth Inclosure map of 1819 (page 9). It shows the open fields and common land of the parish and the roads as re-aligned by the Inclosure Commissioners. The southern boundary of the parish follows the course of the Duke of Northumberland's River which is marked on the map as the Isleworth Mill River. The south-east corner of the parish formed part of Hounslow Heath and was the common land of the parish.

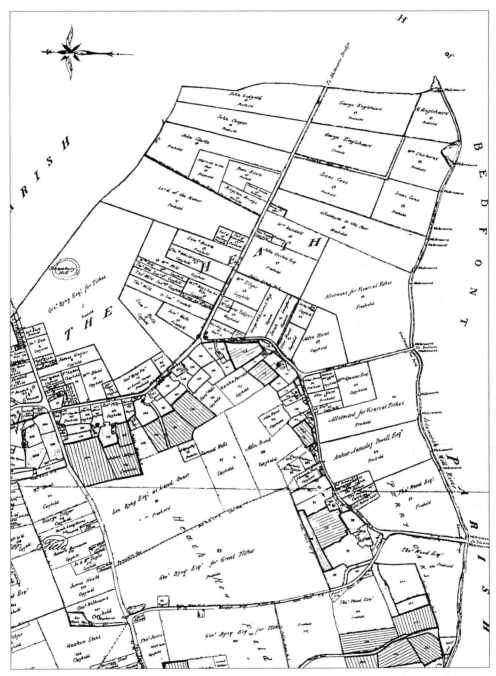

Harmondsworth Inclosure Map, 1819 This map is unusual in that East is shown at the top of the map; it therefore has to be turned through 90° to get the same orientation as the other maps in the book. The original was drawn to a very large scale (18 inches to the mile) and in great detail to illustrate the re-allocation of land within the parish. It shows clearly how the open fields and the common land were split into small enclosed fields. Shasbury Hill of Rocque's map has become Schapsbury Hill but no mention is made of Fern Hill.

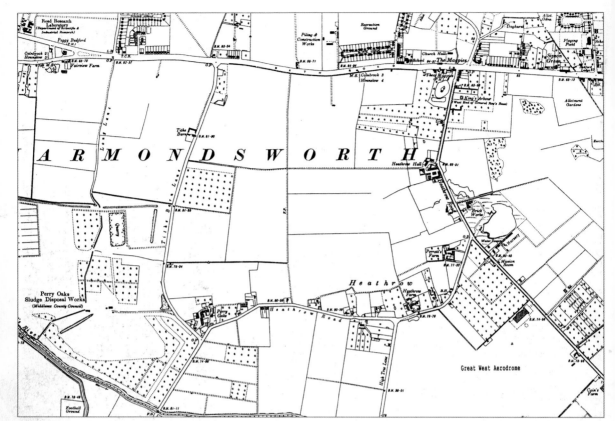

Above: Heathrow, 1935. Comparatively few changes had occurred between the Inclosure of 1819 and 1935. The road layout is identical, the field pattern is still recognisable although some consolidation of the holdings has occurred and a little additional building has taken place. The major change is the presence of the Fairey aerodrome but even that had little impact on the landscape (see page 53). On this map the area of Shasbury/Schapsbury Hill is marked as 'Earthwork' in Gothic letters.

Opposite: Heathrow from the air, 1932. The Fairey aerodrome (see page 53) looking across to the south-west, showing that, except for the large hangar on the north-east corner, the airfield was indistinguishable from the farm land which surrounded it. The road crossing the middle of the photograph in front of the hangar is Cain's Lane. What appears to be a road cutting diagonally across the photograph from the bottom right-hand edge is, in fact, nothing more than a farm track. The hamlet of Heathrow, straggling along Heathrow Road, can be seen in the top right-hand corner. In the far distance Staines Reservoir can be seen on the horizon. (*Photograph courtesy of Aerofilms Ltd*)

Heathrow from the air, 1935. This view is to the north-east with the hangar of the Fairey aerodrome (see page 53) almost in the centre. It gives a good impression of the rural nature of the area at this time with all the land in intensive cultivation. The road running from the bottom right-hand corner is High Tree Lane which crosses the Duke of Northumberland's River and then joins Heathrow Road turning left towards Perry Oaks and right to loop round to join the Bath Road at the Three Magpies (see page 25). (*Photograph courtesy of Quadrant/Flight International*)

Aerial view Heathrow area, 1940. This photograph is one of a series taken on 27 September 1940 by the Luftwaffe during the Battle of Britain. Unfortunately the photograph immediately to the south which was taken on the same occasion is badly obscured by clouds. In this photograph Heathrow lies to the south of the Bath Road which crosses the photograph diagonally at the bottom left-hand corner. The railway line and the loop of the Grand Union canal at Hayes are at the top of the photograph. Towards the top right-hand extremity is the uncompleted alignment of the Parkway at Cranford, work on which had started in 1939 as part of the proposed extensions to Heston aerodrome (see page 48). The Luftwaffe archives are the most complete aerial cover of Britain up to 1940. They were captured at the end of the war and are now in the US National Archives in Washington, which supplied this photograph.

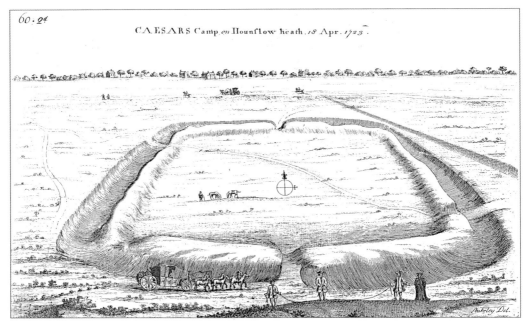

60.2ᵈ

CAESARS Camp on Hounflow heath, 18 Apr. 1723.

Pukeley Del.

Caesar's Camp on Hounslow Heath, 1723. The site of Schapsbury Hill as recorded in 1723 by Stukeley who believed it to be a Roman encampment. The drawing shows how well preserved the earthwork was in 1723 when this part of Hounslow Heath was yet to be enclosed and cultivated.

Reconstruction of Early Iron Age settlement at Heathrow. Drawing by Alan Sorrell, reproduced by permission of the Museum of London. An artist's reconstruction of the site based on information available in the 1960s. Later re-appraisal of the archaeological investigations now suggests that there was a considerable amount of artistic licence in this drawing.

CHAPTER TWO

PRE-HISTORY

Heathrow appears to have been the last of the post-Roman settlements to be formed in Harmondsworth Parish. Harmondsworth itself is in the north-west of the parish and the name is first mentioned in an Anglo-Saxon charter of AD 780 when land in a place called Hermonds was granted by Offa, King of Mercia to his servant Aeldred. By the time of Domesday the name had become Hermondesworde. Sipson, now the second largest settlement in the parish, is first referred to as Subeston in a custumal of the manor of Harmondsworth dating from 1110. Longford is first mentioned in 1337 and the first known reference to Heathrow is in 1453. All the names are of Anglo-Saxon origin and in all cases must have existed long before their first recorded references.

However, long before Saxon times there were settlements in the area. No written record exists but there is plenty of archaeological evidence for human occupation. The most significant in the Heathrow area was the discovery during the construction of the airport of an extensive Iron Age settlement.

The appearance of the area labelled either as Shasbury Hill, Schapsbury Hill or Camp in the maps in the previous section and that of General Roy (page 19) shows that it must have been a significant feature in the flat landscape. The earliest recorded reference to the site is in Camden's *Britanniae* 1586 which says: 'On the north edge of (Hounslow) Heath towards King's Arbour is a Roman camp; a simple work and not large'. It is mentioned again in the map of the Hundred of Isleworth drawn by Moses Glover in 1635. It is just beyond the boundary of Glover's map but, near to the River Crane, he records: 'In this Heathe (i.e. Hounslow Heath) hath many camps bin pitched . . . wherof the forme of two yet in parte remaineth not far beyond this rive. By the name of Shakesbury Hilles'. A suggested derivation of 'Shakesbury' is that it could mean 'robber's camp' and the numerous highwaymen operating on Hounslow Heath could well have used it as a hideout.

The site of Schapsbury Hill was examined by Stukeley in 1723 who believed it to be a Roman encampment. He said it was nearly perfect and sixty paces square, but he did not say why he recognised it as a Roman site or why he called it 'Caesar's Camp'. Stukeley's drawing of the site is shown on page 14. Lysons, writing at the end of the eighteenth century, also mentions the earthwork, stating that it consisted of a single trench about three hundred feet square. It is also mentioned in an account written soon after the Inclosure (1819) which says:

Heathrow is situated to the south of the Bath Road on the margin of Hounslow Heath. At a short distance from this place towards the east, were, until recently, the remains of an ancient camp supposed to be Roman. The vestiges were about 300 feet square and the embankment was defended by a single trench only. The parish of Harmondsworth has recently been enclosed by Act of Parliament and the plough has thrown into furrows the castrametation raised by the Romans in pride of military art.

However, enough survived for it to have been mentioned in the *Victoria County History* which recorded that 'three quarters of a mile north-east of Heathrow, immediately south of

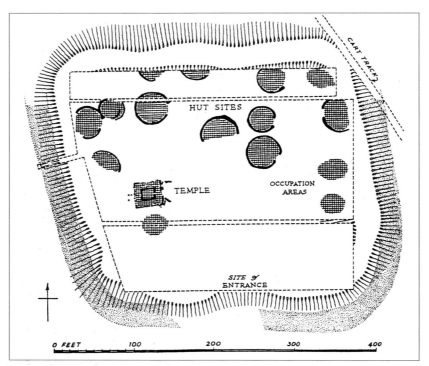

Simplified plan of the Heathrow site as finally excavated by Grimes in 1944, showing the distribution of the hut sites and occupation areas and the position of the temple. (*From Grimes' article in* Archaeology, *Summer, 1948*)

the Bath Road, a small square camp about 380 feet square was extant until the autumn of 1906. It is now ploughed perfectly flat, leaving no trace.' However, it was still significant enough for it to be marked on pre-airport maps.

Grimes reported that, by 1944, the rampart and ditch were much spread and reduced and defied photography from the ground. The bank stood nowhere more than two feet high, its clearest indication being provided by the creep of the plough soil away from its crest, which exposed the light soil of the rampart beneath. The entrance, to the south, was barely discernible. The excavations showed that in the northern half of the enclosure had been a series of eleven huts. This picture of a comparatively small domestic area with a large vacant space probably used as a farmyard and enclosure for cattle was in itself not particularly remarkable. However, it was no ordinary farm. The excavations along the west side, near the base of the bank, were of much greater significance since they revealed the existence of a remarkable rectangular building, 37 × 32 feet in size. This could only have been a temple and of a type earlier than anything previously recorded in this country. It consisted of a central shrine, which must have had solid wooden walls, enclosed by an outer rectangle of thick wooden posts. It was probably covered by a thatched roof that extended downwards from a central ridge-pole to the outer posts. It has been likened to a classical Greek temple, with the stone columns replaced by wooden posts and the stone-walled sanctuary by a structure like a log cabin. This important, indeed unique, site was destroyed and buried under the main runway in 1944.

CHAPTER THREE

GENERAL ROY & THE ORDNANCE SURVEY

There is a little corner of Heathrow which literally helped to put everywhere else in Great Britain on the map. Tucked away off the Bath Road between Heathrow Police Station and the perimeter road is a plaque and a half-buried cannon which commemorate a major breakthrough in the history of mapmaking. Exactly 27,406.19 feet to the south-east there is an identical memorial in the centre of a housing estate in Hampton. The memorials mark the ends of an invisible baseline measured out in 1784, under the supervision of Major General William Roy, across what was then part of Hounslow Heath to establish a baseline of accurately-known length as a prelude to an accurate trigonometrical survey of Great Britain.

Roy chose the site 'because of its vicinity to the capital and the Royal Observatory at Greenwich, its great extent and the extraordinary levelness of the surface without any local obstructions whatever to render the measurement difficult'. One end of his baseline was at King's Arbour, Heathrow and the other at Hampton some five miles away.

There is a popular myth that King's Arbour got its name from the fact that the area was used for stabling the horses of George III, who would not use inns for changing horses on his way to Windsor, but kept an establishment of his own. However, the name was in existence some 200 years before the reign of George III: a Survey of the Manor of Harmondsworth made in 1548 includes a statement that, among other things, Edward Stokewood holds 'One tenement with eight acres of land to the same lying at King's Arbour called Mayhouse Croft, late William Mayhewe'. The name also occurs in the Court Rolls of the Manor for 18 October 1559, when tenants were ordered to make a fence 'from Kynges Arber to Thykattes Gate'.

As the name was well established in the sixteenth Century, this effectively disposes of the myth that the name comes from King George having a stable there. The King referred to in the name was probably a member of the King family whose name occurs in records dating back as far as 1390 relating to Harmondsworth parish. The Harmondsworth Inclosure Award of 1819 records the King as the owner of the piece of land around the cannon at the western end of General Roy's baseline at Heathrow. This is probably the origin of the myth that the land was used by George III for stabling his horses. It was only nine perches (30¼ square yards) in area and thus rather small to be used for stabling.

Arbour may equate with the modern meaning of the word which came into English from the French. It can, however, have a much older origin derived from Old English 'earth-burh' meaning earth fort. As King's Arbour was adjacent to the earthwork mentioned in the previous section, it is quite possible that in this case the Arbour refers to the earthwork.

The origin of Roy's work was in a proposal he submitted in 1763 for a comprehensive 'general survey of the whole Island at public cost'. The proposal was seriously considered but dropped on the grounds that 'it would be a work of much time and labour, and attended with great Expence to the Government'. It was resurrected in 1783 when the Director of the Paris Observatory submitted a paper to George III suggesting the triangulation of south-east England. This, connected to the French network, would provide a means of establishing the relative positions of the Greenwich and Paris Observatories. The paper was forwarded to Sir Joseph Banks, the President of the Royal Society, who immediately proposed that Roy should take charge of the project.

The exact location of the baseline was agreed on the ground by Roy accompanied by Sir Joseph Banks and Charles Blagden. The terminals were at King's Arbour and the Poor House at Hampton; soldiers were used to clear the ground between the two points and generally assist in the survey. The spire of a church, which Roy subsequently discovered was that of Banstead in Surrey, was found to be directly in line with the two ends of the base and provided a useful sighting point.

Rough measurement of the base, using a 100 ft steel chain, started on 16 June 1784 and was completed by the end of the month. On 15 July precise measurements began using wooden (deal) rods but the weather was bad and it soon became apparent that, because of expansion and contraction of the wood with changes in humidity, wooden rods would not be sufficiently accurate. Glass tubes (referred to by Roy as rods) were suggested as a possible alternative by one of Roy's assistants and, somewhat surprisingly, were found to be suitable. It proved possible to obtain glass rods about 20 feet in length and 1 inch in diameter and these rods were mounted in wooden cases. By using specially designed equipment for handling the rods, measurements could be made along the length of the baseline. Work on this started on 17 August and was completed by the end of the month. An amusing aside was Roy's complaint that the carriages passing along the 'Great Road' (the old Staines Road running from Hounslow to Staines) continually interrupted his work. The distance as measured by Roy was 27,404.01 feet (see below and p. 22).

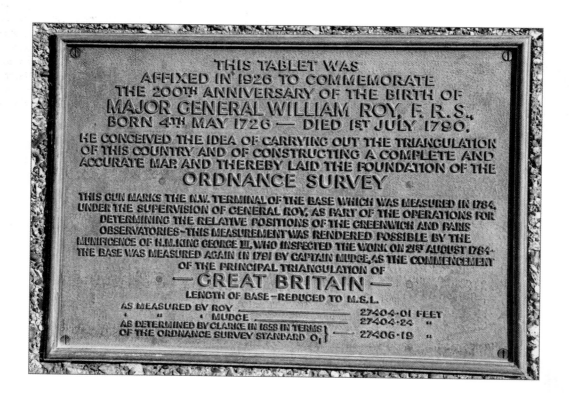

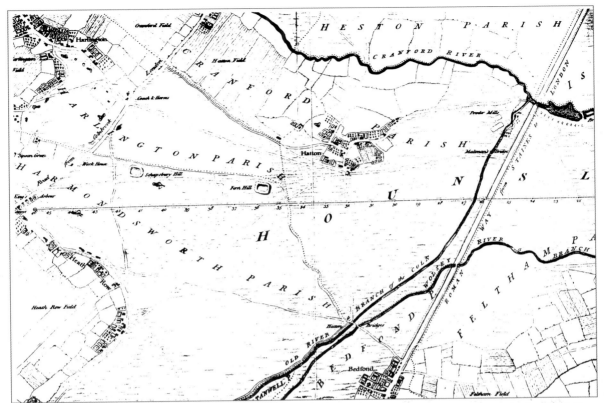

Western end of General Roy's 'Plan shewing the situation of the base measured on Hounslow Heath, 1784'. Roy was judged to have performed his task with 'a labour sufficient to derange a more than common degree of perseverance'. He was therefore presented with the Copley Medal of the Royal Society in 1785 for the 'accurate and satisfactory manner in which he measured a base for operations of Trigonometry, upon Hounslow Heath'. Roy's account of his survey was published in the Proceedings of the Royal Society and the map shown above is a copy of that which accompanies his account. Among other things the map also shows Schapsbury Hill, mentioned in the previous section.

Cannon at each end of the baseline. Roy marked the terminals of the baseline by wooden pipes and waggon wheels sunk into the ground. In 1791 these were found to be in an advanced state of decay and they were replaced by two cannon. Selected from those unfit for service at Woolwich Arsenal, the guns were half-buried in the ground muzzle upwards, one at each end of the baseline. In 1926, at the suggestion of Sir Charles Close (Director General of the Ordnance Survey 1911–22) bronze plaques were fixed to each gun to commemorate the 200th anniversary of Roy's birth. The top photograph shows the cannon at King's Arbour, Heathrow just before its removal in 1943. Unlike its twin, the cannon in the lower photograph at the south-east terminal of the baseline at Hampton has never been removed. When installed in 1791 it stood in open country near the Hampton Poor House but it now stands in Cannon Close, which is a turning off Roy Grove, and is surrounded by a small housing estate.

Unveiling memorial to General Roy, 1967. In 1967 it was realised that something tangible should be done at Heathrow to commemorate Roy's achievement. This took the form of placing a plaque on the wall of Heathrow Police Station, which stands due north of the original site of the cannon. The top photograph shows the plaque being unveiled by General R.C.A. Edge, the Director of the Ordnance Survey on 17 November 1967.

Return of the cannon, 1968. Because it was thought to be a potential danger to aircraft taxi-ing along a proposed runway, the cannon was removed in August 1944 and stored at the Ordnance Survey's temporary headquarters at Chessington. The cannon was returned to Heathrow in 1968 and remained in the Engineering Department of the British Airports Authority until 1972 when it was reinstated in its original position. The photograph shows the cannon awaiting replacement.

Cannon at Heathrow, 1998. The cannon in place with the 1926 plaque now mounted on a sloping concrete plinth on the south side of the cannon. The plaque records the remarkable accuracy of Roy's measurement of the baseline – 27,404.01 feet by his estimation, 27,406.19 feet as determined by the Ordnance Survey.

CHAPTER FOUR

HEATHROW BEFORE THE AIRPORT

Heathrow was the smallest of the four villages and hamlets which together with Longford, Sipson and Harmondsworth make up the parish of Harmondsworth. It is first mentioned in 1453 but was probably in existence well before that date. It lay to the south of the Bath Road in the south-east of the parish on the edge of Hounslow Heath from which it clearly derived its name. In old records, including the Harmondsworth Parish registers, which date from 1680, the name is usually written as one word, the major exception being Rocque's map of 1754 (see page 7) which records it as Heath Row. This variant was used by the Air Ministry, at the time of the seizure of the land during the Second World War to make way for the airport, so as to give the impression that the airport was being built on heathland rather than Grade 1 agricultural land.

Access to Heathrow was via Heathrow Road and Tithe Barn Lane, both of which branched south from the Bath Road (see map on page 10). Heathrow Road left the Bath Road at the Three Magpies (see page 25), and Tithe Barn Lane left at a beauty spot known as 'Shepherd's Pool' about half a mile west of the Three Magpies. Midway between the two roads was a footpath also running due south to Heathrow from the Bath Road which was known as 'Peace Path' – very appropriate at the time but now with ironic overtones.

Heathrow Road ran due south for about half a mile and then forked at Wheatcut Corner. One branch, Cain's Lane, then ran south-east to East Bedfont; the other branch, which retained the name of Heathrow Road, turned in a westerly direction to join Tithe Barn Lane at Perry Oaks. At Perry Oaks the united roads became Oaks Road to run in a south-westerly direction to Stanwell. Another road, High Tree Lane, branched from Heathrow Road between Wheatcut Corner and Perry Oaks to run south to West Bedfont.

The hamlet of Heathrow was scattered along Heathrow Road, with most of its buildings on the west side of the road. Even on the eve of its destruction in 1944 it retained a rural charm, there were very few modern buildings and the whole area was given over to agriculture. It was well-described by Maxwell in *Highwayman's Heath* (1935): 'If you turn down from the Bath Road by the "Three Magpies" you will come upon a road that is as rural as anywhere in England. It is not, perhaps, scenically wonderful but for detachment from London or any urban interests it would be hard to find its equal; there is a calmness and serenity about it that is soothing in a mad rushing world.'

Some forty years later the same area could be described by Hudson and Pettifer in *Diamonds in the Sky* (1979) as follows: 'If there was an international prize for the ugliest landscape, some of the leading contenders would be around a number of the world's leading airports. This is partly because airports have to be situated on flat land which does nothing to hide the acres of concrete and partly because, for safety reasons, tall trees which might soften the skyline are not tolerated. As the more affluent owners flee from the aircraft nuisance – a nuisance which affects eyes, ears and nose – neighbourhoods decline and take on an unloved appearance. What we finish up with, all too frequently, is an unappealing wasteland of warehouses, car parks and poor housing. Anyone who has had the misfortune to spend time around the airports of London, Paris and Chicago will recognise the picture all too well.'

Until 1930 modern developments had made no impact on Heathrow and when they did come they had little effect on the tranquil nature of the area. Agriculture continued to be the dominating industry and this is considered in the next chapter. The first arrival of the twentieth century was the establishment, in 1929, of a small aerodrome by the Fairey Aviation Company of Hayes, which is also considered in a separate chapter. Next on the scene was a sludge disposal works opened at Perry Oaks by Middlesex County Council in 1935 as part of the West Middlesex Drainage Scheme. At about the same time, the Ham River Sand and Gravel Company began excavating gravel from land to the east of Heathrow Road.

The original site of the sludge works at Perry Oaks was 220 acres in extent, on the west side of Tithe Barn Lane, Heathrow. It was purchased by Middlesex County Council on 12 June 1931 for the sum of £33,000 from W. Whittington and Sons, who also occupied Perry Oaks Farm on the opposite side of Tithe Barn Lane. The works still (1999) occupy an enclave of some 250 acres on the western edge of the airport. At the main sewage works at Mogden, sludge is separated from the sewage and, after initial treatment, is pumped over a 7-mile distance to Perry Oaks. The sludge is pumped through a twin 12-inch cast-iron main with an 18-inch cast-iron pipe draining the works back to the Bath Road sewer. The pipes originally followed the route of the Bath Road and the former route of Tithe Barn Lane. Had the route chosen followed a more direct line by going across the fields to Perry Oaks, it is quite probable that it would have rendered the construction of the airport too difficult to achieve.

In 1952, during reconstruction of the northern runway, the opportunity was taken to divert the pipes so that instead of following the route of the former Tithe Barn Lane they continued a little further along the Bath Road and then passed southwards to Perry Oaks at what was then the western end of the runway. The runway has since been extended so that the pipes pass beneath it. However, this presents no problems because, at the time of the diversion, the opportunity was taken to build a subway so that access could be had to the pipes at all times without causing any interference with the operation of the airport.

The Three Magpies, Bath Road, 1951. The last surviving coaching inn on the Bath Road at Heathrow. In the photograph it stands on the western side of the junction of the Bath Road with Heathrow Road. Doghurst Cottages are on the other side of the junction. These were demolished in the early 1950s and the site is now occupied by the Airport Police Station. The Three Magpies has lost its outbuildings and has been extensively restored since the photograph was taken (see page 95). It is an eighteenth-century coaching inn which in 1765 was known as the 'Three Pigeons' and later as the 'Magpie and Pigeon'.

Heathrow School, Bath Road, 1967. The school, for children living in the Heathrow area of Harmondsworth Parish, opened in temporary accommodation in 1874 and moved to its new building in 1877 under the name of 'Heathrow School'. It later changed its name to the more appropriate one of 'Sipson and Heathrow School' as by far the major number of children lived at Sipson. The school on the Bath Road site closed in 1966 and the building was demolished a few years later. Its replacement in Harmondsworth Lane, Sipson illogically reverted to its original name.

Heathrow Hall, 1935. This late eighteenth-century building was the first of the large farmhouses that were dotted along Heathrow Road from the Three Magpies to Perry Oaks. At the time that this photograph was taken it belonged to J.E. Philip & Son, Ltd who farmed much of the land between Heathrow Road and Tithe Barn Lane. It was demolished in 1944 at the beginning of the development of the airport.

Pond at Heathrow, 1927. A number of ponds were scattered along the length of Heathrow Road. They must have started life as small gravel pits but had become an attractive feature and a haunt of herons and kingfishers. This one was directly opposite Heathrow Hall; the little girl is the author's sister.

Perrott's Farm, 1936. This was a half-timbered seventeenth-century farmhouse which had been altered in the late eighteenth century. It stood midway between Palmer's Farm and Heathrow Farm below. The name was probably a corruption of 'Parrott' as it was owned by Martha Parrott at the time of the Harmondsworth Inclosure (1819).

Heathrow Farm, 1936. Dating from the sixteenth-century this farmhouse was situated on the north side of Heathrow Road just past its junction with Cain's Lane. It was a timber-framed building which had been re-faced with brick in the eighteenth century.

Farm Cottages, 1935. Both of these half-timbered cottages had been built in the mid-seventeenth century. They stood on the north side of Heathrow Road about a quarter of a mile west of Heathrow Farm at a point where a footpath known as 'Peace Path' left Heathrow Road and travelled north to join the Bath Road. The name of the path now sounds ironic, but at the time it was most appropriate.

Modern Farmhouses, Cain's Lane, 1944. In contrast to most of the farmhouses, these two were less than twenty years old when they were demolished. The house nearest the camera was known as 'Croft House', built in 1927; the other house, 'Shrub End', was built somewhat later. The occupants were respectively J.E. Wild, his wife and son John in 'Croft House' and David Wild and his family in 'Shrub End'. D.&J. Wild ran a small nursery and market garden (see page 41).

The Cedars, Hatton Road, 1944. Although most of the buildings destroyed to make way for the airport were in the hamlet of Heathrow, parts of Harlington and Hatton shared the same fate. The Cedars was actually in Harlington and was at one time the home of Mary Ann Mitton, who was the inspiration for Charles Dickens' character 'Little Dorrit'. As a friend of the family, Charles Dickens was a regular visitor to the house.

The Dog and Partridge, Hatton Road, 1920s . The only public house that was actually in Heathrow was The Plough and Harrow but two other public houses were to share its fate when all three were demolished to make way for the airport. One was the Old Magpies on the Bath Road (see page 95), the other was the Dog and Partridge which strictly speaking was in Hatton rather than Heathrow; it had stood in Hatton Road about half a mile south of Harlington Corner for over 100 years. A new Dog and Partridge was opened in Edinburgh Drive, Staines in the 1950s: the licence had been held in suspense and transferred to the new public house by way of special removal.

Duke of Northumberland's River, Heathrow. The top photograph, taken in the early 1930s, shows the ford across the river in High Tree Lane. This road ran in a straight line from Heathrow Road to West Bedfont. Half a mile along the lane at a ford marked on maps as 'Goathouse Tree Ford', the road crossed the Duke of Northumberland's River. Goathouse Tree Ford was seldom, if ever, referred to as such and the area of the ford was known locally as High Tree River. It was a local beauty spot popular for picnics where children could safely paddle in the water and fish for 'tiddlers'. The banks were well wooded and on the south side was a pleasant riverside walk to Longford about two miles away. The river is man-made and derives its name from the fact that it supplies Syon House, the home of the Duke of Northumberland, with water. When construction of the airport began in 1944 it was diverted to a more southerly route for about two miles of its length and marker blocks were placed along its former course 'in order that a permanent record of the old bed could be maintained'. Twenty markers, one of which can be seen in the lower photograph, were placed in position. Most of these plaques must have long since disappeared.

Duke of Northumberland's River, Syon Park, 1998. The lake was created in the mid-eighteenth century by Capability Brown, by widening the Duke of Northumberland's river. This resulted in a lake a quarter of a mile long and 40 feet wide. The river is man-made, the channel having been constructed in the mid-sixteenth century to increase the water driving Isleworth Mill and to provide water to Syon House. It runs from the Colne at West Drayton by way of Longford, Heathrow and Bedfont to join the Crane for a short distance at Baber Bridge before proceeding on its own course to Isleworth. It is probable that the river followed the line of a natural watercourse to some degree because in the Heathrow area it formed the boundary between the parishes of Harmondsworth and Stanwell which would have been established well before the sixteenth century. The route of its former channel continued to form the southern boundary of Harmondsworth parish, and hence of the Borough of Hillingdon, until the boundary changes in 1994. Despite its name, the river no longer belongs to the Duke of Northumberland but comes under the control of the National Rivers Authority, which is now part of the Environment Agency. If a fifth terminal at Heathrow were to be built, further diversion of the river would have to be made, with a proposal that it should be piped underground for a considerable distance. It already flows underground beneath the north and south runways but comes up for air in between the two (see page 115).

The Longford River. The top photograph shows the King's Bridge over the Longford River on the old Bath Road at Longford. The middle of the bridge on each of its four sides has a plaque with the monogram 'W R 1834' underneath the royal crown. The bottom photograph shows the 'Long Water' at Hampton Court which is supplied by the Longford River. The river was dug on the orders of Charles I who, in 1638, commissioned an inquiry into 'how the waters of the Colne could be brought over Hounslow Heath into the Park' so as to improve the water supply of Hampton Court. The course of the river was changed in the 1940s as a result of the construction of Heathrow Airport so that at one point it goes underground and shares a channel with the Duke of Northumberland's River. The bridge and river are still Crown property and the Crown Estates are concerned that the proposals to run the river underground for an even greater distance, to allow for the construction of a fifth terminal at Heathrow, would adversely affect the quality of the water at Hampton Court.

MIDDLESEX COUNTY COUNCIL

INAUGURATION

OF THE

WEST MIDDLESEX
MAIN DRAINAGE SCHEME

BY

THE RIGHT HONOURABLE SIR KINGSLEY WOOD, M.P.
Minister of Health

Inauguration of the West Middlesex Main Drainage Scheme. The sludge works at Perry Oaks forms part of the West Middlesex Main Drainage Scheme, which was officially opened on 23 October 1936 by Sir Kingsley Wood, who was Minister of Health at that time. The main works is at Mogden in the middle of what, even then, was a highly populated area and which would not have tolerated a sludge works as a neighbour. The sludge was therefore pumped from Mogden to a remote area of Heathrow some seven miles away where the settling lagoons would present less of a problem.

When it arrives at Perry Oaks, the sludge has a solids content of about 2 per cent, and, in the original process, it was pumped into lagoons where the solid matter slowly separated under gravity and most of the water drained off. After settling in the lagoons, the volume and weight of the sludge was much reduced and it then had a solids content which had been raised from its initial value of about 2 per cent to a solids content of 10 per cent. It had also been changed into a product which was easy to handle and no longer offensive. The dried sludge was then removed in road tankers and spread, as a fertiliser, on agricultural land.

The method was a very cheap and efficient method of treating waste but suffered from the fact that it occupied a large area of land. Because of this, and the pressures to develop the site for the extension of the airport, in the mid-1990s Thames Water transferred its mode of operation entirely to a mechanical process for de-watering the sludge. This method requires only 10 per cent of the space taken up by the original method.

Aerial view of the Perry Oaks sludge works, 1936. A view of the works looking across to the south-west. The road running across the bottom left-hand corner is Tithe Barn Lane, which gave access to the works. The buildings in the distance at the top of the photograph are in Stanwell Moor.

CHAPTER FIVE

AGRICULTURE IN THE HEATHROW AREA

INTRODUCTION

Harmondsworth Parish was enclosed in 1819. Before this, the area bounded by Heathrow Road, Tithe Barn Lane and the Bath Road was one of the open fields of the parish, known as Heathrow Field. The area to the south and east of Heathrow Road was the common land of the parish and formed the western edge of Hounslow Heath. Heathrow, as its name suggests, was on the edge of the Heath bordered, on the northern and western sides, by the open arable fields of Harmondsworth Parish.

After the Inclosure the opportunity existed to upgrade the quality of the land and despite the proximity to Hounslow Heath with its notorious connotations of sterility, the whole area developed into high-quality agricultural land. The brick-earth soils which cover most of the area are light brown silty clays liable to dry into clods, but friable when moist and, with liming and manuring, are capable of giving excellent results. The Land Utilisation Survey Report of 1937 described them as being 'some of the best in England and they are, and have been, extensively used for market gardening, although they are well-suited to almost any type of farming. In the national interest it is, therefore, a matter for regret that so much development of an urban and suburban character has been permitted to take place on this highly productive land.'

The report went on to lament the fact that 'at least four aerodromes have been recently established in the region, three of them involving the conversion of excellent market-gardening land into grassland of little agricultural value'. The four aerodromes referred to must have been Hanworth, Heston, Fairey's at Heathrow and Hawker's at Langley. Although regrettable, the loss of land to the Fairey airfield had little effect on the rural nature of the area and the Heathrow area represented the last significant tract of Grade 1 agricultural land in West Middlesex still in use for intensive production at the outbreak of war in 1939.

FRUIT FARMING

By the latter half of the nineteenth century West Middlesex had become an important fruit-growing area. The orchards planted in this period were mixed so that within one orchard there would have been apples, pears and plums of many different varieties. In addition to tree fruit, a large variety of soft fruit – such as raspberries, strawberries, gooseberries – were grown; in many cases the soft fruit was grown under the trees in the orchards.

MARKET GARDENING

Improvements in communications and the growth of London led, in West Middlesex, to a gradual change to market gardening from other forms of farming. It became easier to transport the products of this type of farming from more distant parts, while the growth of London's population increased the demand for market gardening produce, especially that of a more perishable nature. Thus, by the time that it was overwhelmed by the airport, West Middlesex had become an important market gardening area with Heathrow itself virtually in the centre of what remained of the Thames Valley Market Gardening Plain (see map on page 38). As already discussed, the reason for this was that the brick-earth soils of the Heathrow area, by virtue of their texture, topography and drainage, were ideally suited to intensive agriculture. But apart from this, the inherent fertility of the soils had been greatly improved over the years by the addition of huge quantities of stable-waste arising from the immense horse population of London.

Up to the end of the nineteenth century all the traffic in London was horse-drawn and even in the 1930s horse-drawn transport was a still-significant feature. The disposal of the horse-droppings would have been a serious problem had it not been for the fact that the market gardening wagons trundling into London each day with fresh fruit and vegetables were able to make the return journey loaded with manure. The amount of stable manure used by the market gardeners was immense and the Land Utilisation Survey reported that, even in the early 1930s when the amount of stable manure available was rapidly declining, an annual application of 20 to 40 tons per acre was not considered excessive.

As the horse population declined, alternatives had to be found and a popular one was actually situated at Heathrow in the form of sewage sludge from the Perry Oaks sludge works. An annual application of as much as 50 tons of dried sewage sludge per acre was used on some market gardens. A surprise feature of this was that tomato plants became quite common field-weeds, as tomato seeds are able to survive human digestion and disposal through the sewage works.

The LUS report pointed out that the market gardeners could justifiably claim that they actually made their soils, by a process which took many years, and few of them had anything to learn from soil scientists. They applied lime, chalk, farmyard manure, sewage sludge and phosphates and used appropriate ploughing techniques to bring their soils into the right condition to give the best yields of a succession of crops. The improvement in soil conditions was to such a degree that, valued in terms of capital improvements, the soil was often of greater value than the land on which it rested.

The market garden crops grown in the area included cabbages of various kinds, cauliflowers, lettuces, spinach, beetroot, turnips, parsnips, carrots, radishes, onions, leeks, artichokes, potatoes, marrows, peas, all types of beans and produce such as rhubarb, sea-kale and tomatoes which were grown in cold frames, glasshouses and forcing sheds.

THE EFFECT OF THE AIRPORT ON FARMING

According to the Greater London Development Plan of 1944 (GLDP), 'Although the airport (Heathrow) is on land of first-rate agricultural quality, it is felt, after careful consideration and thorough weighing-up of all the factors, that the sacrifice for the proposed purpose of the airport is justified.' The GLDP was written after the decision to construct the airport had been made and was a government-sponsored publication. As Mandy Rice-Davies might have remarked, 'They would say that, wouldn't they.'

In fact no consideration was given to the unique agricultural importance of the Heathrow area. This was the more reprehensible because Heathrow was at the very centre of the Thames

Valley Market Gardening Plain. At a time of severe food shortages and stringent rationing this important market gardening area close to London should have been regarded as a valuable national resource and not one to be destroyed for the construction of an airport that could have been sited on land of lower agricultural potential.

The folly of destroying the valuable market garden land for the construction of an airport was well described by Dudley Stamp, the leading authority on land use and classification at the time. In a separate report included in the GLDP, he wrote: 'The brick-earth is a magnificent soil – easily worked, adequately watered, of high natural fertility and capable of taking and holding manure. It is a soil fit to be ranked with the world's very best. . . . In addition to the destruction of this good land by gravel digging, a further using up has recently been made manifest where huge areas are taken for the construction of the airport. Was there ever such a profligate waste?'

The construction of the airport in 1944 initially involved the misappropriation of 1300 acres of agricultural land – 15 per cent of the agricultural land in south-west Middlesex. Twenty growers were displaced either wholly or partly from their holdings. Subsequent airport-related developments have since made further inroads into the agricultural land in the area and the once-prosperous West Middlesex market gardening industry has been virtually destroyed in less than a generation.

The ultimate folly is that Heathrow is still a source of supply of fruit and vegetables, which are now imported to Britain by air from all over the world. There may be some justification for importing products which cannot be grown in this country, but to import vegetables that we could easily grow ourselves does not make sense except in a world where environmental costs are always ignored. In the long run it is obviously not even economically sustainable, and it is morally questionable to import food from Third World countries which suffer from food shortages and which distort their economies to provide food for countries which could easily grow their own.

Ploughing match at Heathrow, 1935. See caption on p. 42.

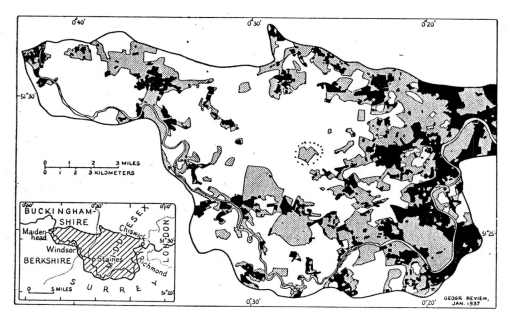

The Thames Valley Market Gardening Plain, 1932. In the upper map the solid line delineates the area of first-class arable soil which constituted the region. The areas in non-agricultural use in 1914 are shown in black. The stippled areas are those that passed out of agricultural use between 1914 and 1936. The Fairey airfield (see page 53) in the centre of the map has been circled by a dotted line. Very little of this area of Grade 1 agricultural land is now used for agriculture. 'The lower map shows a section of the region in which modern building has only just begun to disturb the purely rural landscape, whose almost level surface is entirely devoted to market gardening and is divided into very large fields by the removal of hedges. Cultivation is practised under the trees of the few remaining orchards, the majority of which have been removed in favour of uninterrupted cultivation. The farmsteads are large and the big storage barns attached to each swell the size of the neat little hamlets; the large building on the north of Sipson Lane is a glasshouse used in conjunction with one of the market-gardens.' (Excerpt from the Report of the Land Utilisation Survey of Middlesex and the London Region, 1937). Key: A (MG) – Market Gardening; G – Orchard; G (A) – Orchards under which a ground crop is cultivated; G (M) – Grass Orchards.

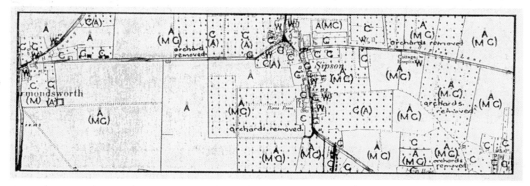

Farm buildings at Sipson Farm, *c.* 1910. Messrs Wild and Robbins of Sipson Farm was the largest market gardening enterprise in the Heathrow area. The size and construction of their farm buildings give a good indication of the prosperity of farming in West Middlesex. The farm was badly disrupted by the construction of the M4 motorway and of the airport spur in the early 1960s but carried on until 1970. The farm buildings shown in the photograph were demolished to make way for housing development about 10 years later.

Derelict farmland, Sipson Farm, 1996. A good illustration of the blighting effect of the airport on much of the land in the surrounding area. The land is Grade 1 agricultural land and there is no good reason why it should not be farmed except that, whereas its agricultural value can be reckoned in thousands of pounds, its value if planning permission were to be given for an airport-related development would be in millions. Not surprisingly, many landowners prefer to leave the land in a derelict condition in the hope that this will increase their chances of gaining planning permission. The sad remains of the glasshouse, mentioned in the Land Utilisation Report on the previous page, can just be seen in the middle distance. Behind this is the grotesque bulk of the Forte Crest Hotel (see page 93).

LOT EIGHT (*Coloured Green on Plan*).

COMPRISES AN EXCEEDINGLY VALUABLE

Freehold Property

A CONSIDERABLE PORTION OF WHICH IS PLANTED WITH FRUIT TREES,

AND IS CONSIDERED ABSOLUTELY

The Finest Fruit Plantation in the District,

KNOWN AS

"Lord's Field,"

SITUATE AT

HEATHROW, in the Parish of HARMONDSWORTH, Middlesex,

CONTAINING ABOUT

57a. Or. 36p.,

Abutting on the Main Road from WEST DRAYTON to BEDFONT.

Bounded on the North by the Property of A. Chantler, Esq., Mr. T. Wild and Earl Strafford; on the East by the Parish of Harlington; on the South by the Property of Mr. H. Barnfield and the Harmondsworth Poor's Land; and on the West by the said West Drayton and Bedfont Road, to which it has

An Extensive Frontage of about 750 feet.

About 26a. 1r. 17p. are planted with Top and Under Fruit Trees of the very best known marketable kinds, in full bearing and in excellent condition, the remainder being

OPEN · MARKET · GARDEN · GROUND

OF MOST PRODUCTIVE QUALITY.

Let on Lease to Mr. Charles Glenie for 14 years from the 29th September, 1898, at the reduced Rental of

PER £206 : 10 : 0 ANN.

The Property, which is in first-class heart and condition, is Tithe Free and Land Tax Redeemed, and is sold subject to the said Lease modified as to Rental as mentioned in the 4th Condition of Sale.

Sale of orchard and market gardening land at Heathrow, 1898. The land in question was on the east side of Cain's Lane and the details refer to the finest fruit plantation in the district. At the time much of the Heathrow area was used for fruit farming. The presence of the orchards greatly enhanced the flat landscape and was the subject of much favourable comment: for example, Stephen Springall in his *Country Rambles around Uxbridge* (1907) declares 'Fruit trees we shall find to obtain in this neighbourhood for all round Harmondsworth, Harlington, Sipson and Heathrow are thousands and thousands of plum, cherry, pear, apple and damson trees in addition to innumerable bushes of currant and gooseberry which grow and flourish to perfection in the flat and open country.'

The farm of D. & J. Wild, Cain's Lane, Heathrow, 1944. This photograph, looking in an easterly direction, was taken from the bedroom window of David Wild's house (Shrub End – see page 28) shortly before the farm was requisitioned by the Air Ministry in the summer of 1944. The packing shed and greenhouses were removed to their new farm near Colchester and the value of these was deducted from the compensation they received.

Sale leaflet for bedding plants, Wild's Farm, Heathrow, 1938. Most of the agricultural activities at Heathrow were given over to intensive market gardening but horticulture of crops under glass also played a significant part. Some of the glasshouses of Wild's Farm can be seen in the top photograph. The largest glasshouses in the area were at Sipson Farm where Wild and Robbins (the Wilds of Heathrow and Sipson were distantly related) grew more exotic crops such as grapes and peaches.

D. J. & J. E. WILD,

Heathrow,

WEST DRAYTON, MIDDLESEX.

List of Spring Bedding Plants.

STOCK. Red, White, Pink, Mauve and Mixed.
ASTER. Rose, White and Mixed
ANTIRRHINUM. Crimson, Flame and Pink
MARIGOLD, French and African
CALENDULA, Radio
HELICHRYSOM, Everlasting Flower
STATICE, Blue, Rose and Yellow
NICOTIANA, Tobacco Plant
SCABIOUS, Pink and Mixed
BALSAM, Mixed
PETUNIA, Mixed
ALYSSUM, White

ALL AT
1/6
PER BOX
OF
50 PLANTS.

	PER DOZ.
GERANIUMS (Potted), Red, Pink and Ivy	4/-
PANSIES, Wine Shades and Yellow	1/-
CHRYSANTHS. & DWARF DAHLIAS	1/-
MARROWS (Potted)	3/-
TOMATOES, Three Varieties	6d.

Smallholdings, Burrows Hill Close Estate. After the First World War the Middlesex County Council acquired land between Heathrow and Stanwell Moor on the north side of Spout Lane which was laid out as small holdings each with its own bungalow and plot of land. Spout Lane originally ran from Stanwell Moor to Oaks Road, Stanwell and its eastern end was cut off in the 1940s in the second phase of the construction of the airport. Soon after, what remained was cut in two by the construction of Stanwell Moor Road. The eastern part was then renamed Burrows Hill Lane and the smallholdings in this area are known as the Burrows Hill Close Estate.

Ploughing Match at Heathrow, 1935. The rural nature of the area meant that Heathrow was the natural choice for staging the annual ploughing matches organised by the Middlesex Agricultural and Growers' Association. These were held in early autumn directly after the harvest. The last match ever to be held was the ninety-ninth which took place on 28 September 1937 on the farm of J.E. Philp and Son of Heathrow Hall on land in Tithe Barn Lane, Heathrow.

CHAPTER SIX

AVIATION IN WEST MIDDLESEX, 1914–44

The fact that the gravel and overlying soils that cover most of West Middlesex were deposited under water means that the land is flat and level in character with a general slope of no more than ten feet per mile. This makes it ideally suitable not only for agriculture but also for aviation. In addition it is close to London with relatively good communications and in the early twentieth century it had a low population density. It was not therefore surprising that within a few years the outbreak of the First World War, aviation interests should seek to establish airfields in the area. The map on the next page shows the location of the four airfields that form the subject of this chapter.

HOUNSLOW HEATH AERODROME

Part of Hounslow Heath was used as an airfield by the Royal Flying Corps during the First World War. The aerodrome was first used by the RFC as a base for anti-Zeppelin spotter aircraft and later as a pilot training airfield. At the end of the war, it was taken over as London's first airport on 1 April 1919 and, soon after, the first regular flights from London to Paris began from the airfield. The first-ever flight from England to Australia took off from the aerodrome on 12 November 1919 and arrived at Darwin on 10 December 1919 having completed the journey in 27 days, 20 hours, 20 minutes. The airfield closed in 1920 and all the services were transferred to Croydon.

LONDON AIR PARK, HANWORTH

The association of Hanworth with aviation started in 1917 when Hanworth Park was used by Whitehead Aircraft Ltd of Feltham from which to fly their aircraft for test flights and deliveries. With the end of the war all flying activities came to an end and did not resume until 1928 when 229 acres of Hanworth Park were laid out as an airfield by National Flying Services Ltd with Hanworth House serving as the club house for the private airfield. About 1933 the General Aircraft Company came to Feltham and used the air park during the Second World war for their Hamilcar gliders and other planes. Flying ceased in 1946 because of Hanworth's proximity to Heathrow. In 1959 it became a public park owned by the local council.

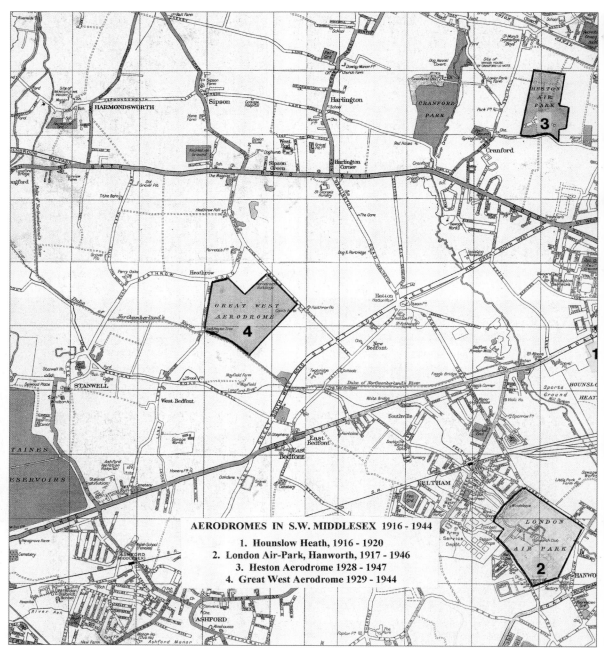

AERODROMES IN S.W. MIDDLESEX 1916 - 1944

1. Hounslow Heath, 1916 - 1920
2. London Air-Park, Hanworth, 1917 - 1946
3. Heston Aerodrome 1928 - 1947
4. Great West Aerodrome 1929 - 1944

Aerodromes in West Middlesex, 1916–44. This map shows the location of the four airfields that were established in West Middlesex between 1916 and 1944 at Hounslow, Hanworth, Heston and Heathrow respectively. Hounslow Heath airfield, which was the first to be established, had a very short life and had closed by 1920. One, the Great West Aerodrome, belonging to the Fairey Aviation Company, became the nucleus of Heathrow Airport and the other two had to close soon after because of their close proximity to the newly-established airport.

Hounslow Heath aerodrome. The top photograph shows the aerodrome just before it closed in 1920. A plaque to commemorate the airfield was erected by the former Borough of Heston and Isleworth and unveiled by the Mayor of the newly created Borough of Hounslow in January 1966. It stands in the Staines Road opposite The Hussar and is shown in the lower photograph which was taken in 1998.

Flying at Heathrow, Cain's Lane, *c.* 1903. This is probably the earliest record of any aerial activities at Heathrow. It shows a lighter-than-air balloon which had made a forced landing at Cain's Farm. Twenty-five years later the Fairey Aviation Company opened its airfield in Cain's Lane close to where the balloon had crash-landed.

Flight over Ashford, 1911. In 1911 the appearance of an aeroplane in the Heathrow area was such a phenomenon that this photograph was published as a picture postcard. The flight probably took place over Shortwood Common.

The *Graf Zeppelin* at Hanworth, 1932. Hanworth is best remembered, locally, by the visit of this famous airship in 1932. The top photograph shows the airship coming in to land and it can be seen on the ground in the bottom photograph which gives a good indication of its immense size. After returning to Germany the airship, which had been built in 1928, went on to cross the Atlantic on commercial flights until the outbreak of war in 1939. It was the most successful airship ever to be built and during its career, unlike the ill-fated *Hindenburg*, it travelled more than 1 million miles without serious incident. It was destroyed during the Second World War.

HESTON AERODROME

This airfield started life as a private airfield in 1928 when a private company – Airwork Ltd – bought 170 acres of land on the north side of Cranford Lane between the still-rural villages of Heston and Cranford. The official opening took place on 6 July 1929. By 1934 Airwork Ltd was losing money on its operations from Heston aerodrome and, when it decided to sell, it seemed likely that the land would be developed for housing. At that time civil aviation interests were overseen by the Air Ministry which was soon put under pressure to buy the airfield and the surrounding open land so as to develop Heston as a viable alternative to Croydon – then the main civil airport in Britain – which was becoming too small to accommodate the expected increase in air transport.

The Air Ministry was very reluctant to become the owner and its first response was to try to persuade the County Councils of London and Middlesex and the Borough Council of Heston and Isleworth to take over Heston as a municipal aerodrome to be run by the three local authorities. The Councils' responses were that if it was to be a national/international airport they could not see why they should be expected to bear the costs of development.

For example, the Aerodromes Committee of the Middlesex County Council resolved, at its meeting on 19 June 1936, that it 'was unable to recommend the Council to proceed with the purchase of Heston airport either solely or in conjunction with the LCC'. Interestingly, at that meeting the Committee also considered and rejected an alternative proposal put forward by the Valuation Officers of the MCC and the LCC to locate a municipal aerodrome at Harmondsworth near the Perry Oaks Sludge Works, which the officers 'considered to be more satisfactory than Heston from all points of view. It was larger in area and would be less costly to develop; it could be extended by a further area of approx. 300 acres and the Southern Railway Stations at Feltham and Ashford were nearby affording good communications with London.'

The action of the local councils in rejecting the Air Ministry's proposals put further pressure on the Ministry to acquire Heston. This was exemplified by an article in the *Daily Telegraph* in August 1936, which is reproduced later. The Air Ministry was unmoved and declared in September 1936 that 'there was no case for the purchase of Heston as a state-owned civil airport'. However, pressure continued to be exerted and came to a head in October when the owners of the airfield lost patience and put it up for sale. The Air Ministry decided, in November, to purchase the airfield and much of the surrounding open land for the construction of an airport as a replacement for Croydon. Oddly enough, soon after the Air Ministry had acquired Heston, Middlesex County Council had a change of mind and urged the Air Ministry to develop Heathrow by expanding the Fairey aerodrome instead of developing Heston. The Air Ministry refused to consider such a proposal, because of the difficulties in acquiring the land, and went ahead with its plans for Heston. Expansion of the airfield at a cost of £2.5m was envisaged which involved the acquisition of land between the existing airfield and the Bath Road and what has since become the Parkway, increasing the area to 814 acres; the construction of a concrete runway 2000 yards in length; and adding extra terminal capacity. Soon after, Heston aerodrome became famous as the airfield to which Neville Chamberlain returned in 1938 after his meeting with Hitler in Munich.

Heston Aerodrome in 1931. The view is towards the north-west; the road in the bottom left-hand corner is Cranford Lane, which was the only access by road to the airfield. If the extensions proposed in 1938 had been realised the airfield would have extended beyond Cranford Lane as far south as the Bath Road (see map on page 51).

Heston Aerodrome, 1935. Looking almost due south, the access from Cranford Lane can be clearly seen with open farmland between Cranford Lane and the Bath Road, which is at the top of the photograph. This farmland was due to be swallowed up by the proposed extensions but, remarkably, most of it still (1999) survives in agricultural production. (*Photograph courtesy of RAF Museum, Reference No. 5528 – 4*)

Arrival of Neville Chamberlain at Heston, 1938. Neville Chamberlain's flights to Munich in September 1938 were one of the first examples of 'shuttle diplomacy'. In all, he made three flights from Heston for his meetings with Hitler. On the last occasion he returned with the notorious treaty signed by Hitler promising 'peace in our time'. The photograph shows him reading the statement to the large crowd which had gathered to welcome him. (*Photograph courtesy of RAF Museum, Reference No 5808 – 7*)

THE DAILY TELEGRAPH, TUESDAY.

HESTON AIRPORT IN DANGER

BUILDERS THREATEN EXTENSION PLANS

INTENDED RUNWAY OF 1,700 YARDS

By Major C. C. TURNER,
" Daily Telegraph " Air Correspondent

Unless immediate action is taken, land on which Heston airport could be extended will pass into the hands of the builder.

London would thus sacrifice an opportunity to possess an airport comparable to those of Berlin, Paris, Amsterdam, and Frankfurt.

London's existing aerodromes will soon be unable to cope with the demands made upon them. Croydon is inadequate. Even when Fairlop, the new aerodrome projected in Essex, is ready, Heston will still be needed.

Heston was the first British aerodrome to instal the blind approach and wireless beam system.

CONTINENTAL AIRPORTS

But it is too small. Its maximum measurements are 960 by 700 yards. Measurements of some of the bigger European airports are : ·

BERLIN.—Runways of 2,750 and 1,730 yards.

FRANKFURT.—700 acres for airships and aeroplanes and runways of 2,432 and 1,716 yards.

PARIS (Le Bourget).—Runways of 1,970 and 1,313 yards in an area of 500 acres, to be extended to 1,000 acres.

AMSTERDAM.—Now being extended to 1,640 by 1,250 yards.

Plans for the extension of Heston have been worked out in detail. They involve the diversion of a right of way and the acquisition of additional areas. This work is beyond the scope of a private company.

If the extension scheme were saved Heston could have a runway of 1,700 yards in a few months.

Moreover, the proposed new western exit from London, the widening of the Great West-road, and the removal of the airport buildings to a position close to the Great Western Railway would make Heston one of the most accessible airports in the world. It would be within 18 minutes of Paddington.

How successful the development of the aerodrome has been is shown by the fact that the present rent roll amounts to £10,000 a year.

All over the country opportunities for providing airports are being lost, and every year increases the cost.

HESTON airport, showing proposed extensions. The areas east and south of the present aerodrome are in danger of being built over.

Heston Aerodrome, showing the proposed extensions. Criticism of the Air Ministry's attitude to civil aviation reached a peak in 1936 when Heston airport was put up for sale by its owners and the open land around it seemed likely to be developed for housing. The airfield had started life as a private airfield in 1928 but by 1935 its owners had decided to sell it. The Air Ministry was soon put under pressure to buy the airfield and the surrounding open land so as to develop Heston as a viable alternative to Croydon. This was exemplified by the article in the *Daily Telegraph* in August 1936, which is reproduced here.

Evening Standard, Friday, April 28, 1939

LONDON VILLAGE DOOMED
Cranford Must Make Room for Airport

CRANFORD RECTORY.

Evening Standard Reporter

PRETTY little Cranford, one of the last remaining villages in the London area, is doomed.

Severed by the modern Bath road, half of it is already engulfed by the spread of the metropolis. Now most of the other half, with its High-street, its farms and market gardens that have been hardly disturbed for centuries, is to be pulled down to make more room for Heston Airport.

The Rectory, the village stores, two farms and two inns are among the hundred houses acquired by the Air Ministry and earmarked for demolition. Already, as I walked through the place to-day, workmen were cutting down fruit trees.

Cranford is mentioned in Domesday.

Cranford's pride is its beautiful little church, in the park, Saxon and eighteenth century, with its interesting monuments—one particularly lovely thing in marble commemorating a relative of Henry VIII.'s Queen, Anne Boleyn.

The extension plan spares the church, but dooms the delightful fourteenth century rectory

Tentlow Farm has already gone, and Mr. Rawle, of the Park Farm, must yield possession in September. His creeper-covered farm-house is some 200 years old.

Touch of Irony

"The land," he said, " is the best agricultural land in Middlesex."

And indeed it is ironic that while economists deplore the decay of British agriculture, it should be common knowledge in the village that the Air Ministry has been paying £700 to £800 an acre for Cranford's splendid agricultural land in order to destroy it for an airfield.

Other local land that fetched £36 an acre a few years ago has been acquired at £53 an acre.

The Jolly Carpenters Inn, which has been in the Clements family for 70 years, is coming down, and Mr. "Bill" Clements, who was born in a house opposite 75 years ago, and his daughter, Mrs. Wingrove, who holds the licence to-day, must find another home.

Cranford's oldest inhabitant, 80-year-old Polly Twidale, just escapes—she lives in the bisected half of the village. But the Queen's Head, with Queen Elizabeth's profile embossed on its front, has been taken over.

"A shock to me," said the licensee, Mr. E. C. Slann. "The brewers spent £14,000 on rebuilding the house eight years ago, and I took it thinking I was going to finish my days in peace here."

MR. RAWLE

Threatened demolition of Cranford. This excerpt from the *Evening Standard* of 28 April 1939 refers to the demolitions that would take place as a result of the proposal to extend Heston aerodrome. Work on the plan actually started in 1939 with the demolition of some buildings in Cranford and laying out the route of the Parkway. It had not progressed very far when war broke out in September and the plans for the construction of a new civil airport for London were seemingly abandoned for the duration of the war. But for this, Heston would have become the largest civil airport in Britain by the end of 1941.

THE GREAT WEST AERODROME

Charles Richard Fairey (1887–1956) began his aeronautical career by selling model aircraft to Gamages of High Holborn. In 1915 he formed his own company – the Fairey Aviation Company – which initially operated from factory premises in Clayton Road, Hayes. Fairey also bought a field in Harlington, bounded by Station Road, North Hyde Road and Dawley Road. The Harlington site was subsequently developed as the headquarters and factory of the company. A few flights were made from the field at Harlington but it was not really suitable and, from 1917, Northolt aerodrome became Fairey's test-flying base. Northolt was owned and operated by the Air Ministry, which in 1928 served notice on the company to vacate its leased premises, which meant that it was forced to find another site for its experimental and production test-flying.

The new site had to be within a reasonable distance of Hayes and, according to Peter Masefield, the site eventually purchased was chosen because Norman Macmillan, Fairey's test pilot, remembered that a few years earlier in 1925, he had had to make a forced landing in a field at Heathrow and later managed to take off again without difficulty. He was impressed by the flatness and stability of the ground so, when he learned that Fairey's were to leave Northolt, he suggested that somewhere in the vicinity of this field would be an excellent choice for a new aerodrome. He made some aerial surveys of the area which confirmed his original impressions and Fairey's then made contact with the owner of the field and owners of adjacent fields. The maps on the next two pages show the extent of the purchases and the area of the airfield.

Preparation of the airfield, c. 1930. The fields purchased by the company were consolidated and initially sown with couch grass. Later the airfield was levelled and re-grassed by the specialist company, C.P. Hunter and laid out as an area of high-quality turf which was used for the first time in the late summer of 1930. The photograph shows some of the grass-sowing operations in progress.

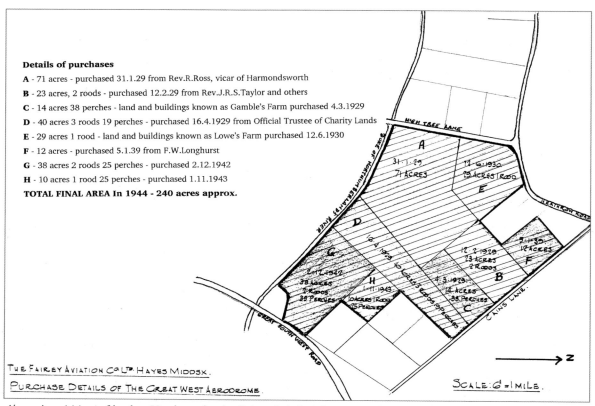

Details of purchases

A - 71 acres - purchased 31.1.29 from Rev.R.Ross, vicar of Harmondsworth

B - 23 acres, 2 roods - purchased 12.2.29 from Rev.J.R.S.Taylor and others

C - 14 acres 38 perches - land and buildings known as Gamble's Farm purchased 4.3.1929

D - 40 acres 3 roods 19 perches - purchased 16.4.1929 from Official Trustee of Charity Lands

E - 29 acres 1 rood - land and buildings known as Lowe's Farm purchased 12.6.1930

F - 12 acres - purchased 5.1.39 from F.W.Longhurst

G - 38 acres 2 roods 25 perches - purchased 2.12.1942

H - 10 acres 1 rood 25 perches - purchased 1.11.1943

TOTAL FINAL AREA In 1944 - 240 acres approx.

THE FAIREY AVIATION CO LTD HAYES MIDDSX.

PURCHASE DETAILS OF THE GREAT WEST AERODROME

SCALE: 6' = 1 MILE.

Above: Acquisition of land at Heathrow by the Fairey Aviation Company, 1929–43. The first land to be bought was a 71-acre plot in the care of the vicar of Harmondsworth, being held by him in lieu of the vicarial tithes of the parish. The Church Commissioners no doubt thought that the money released by the sale could be invested and produce an income for the vicar and his successors that would at least be equal to any rent they could obtain from the land. Would they have proceeded with this seemingly innocuous transaction if they had known that it would eventually lead to a threat to the very existence of the parish of Harmondsworth and the possible destruction of its ancient church? Adjacent plots were bought at much the same time, so that by the middle of 1929 the Company had possession of nearly 180 acres of land in Cain's Lane, Heathrow for which £28,000 had been paid. The last plot was acquired in November 1943 only two months before the company first learned that it was to lose the land it had so patiently acquired.

Opposite: Location of the Fairey Aerodrome. The map shows the extent of the airfield in about 1939 after an additional hangar had been erected but before the company had acquired the additional land to take the boundaries up to the Great South West Road (see previous map).

PRIVATE AERODROME

HEATHROW
(The Great West Aerodrome)

Classification :

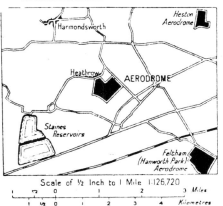

Telegrams :
" Airily Hayes
Middx."

Telephone :
Feltham 2253.

Scale of ½ Inch to 1 Mile 1:126,720

Lat. 51° 27′ 55″ N., **Long.** 00° 26′ 50″ W.

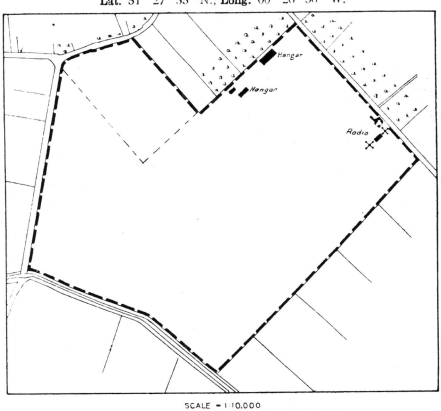

SCALE = 1:10,000

The Heathrow site was as close to the Hayes factory as was Northolt and proved to be just as convenient. It also had the advantage that the company held the freehold – little did Fairey know that the Air Ministry, having expelled him from Northolt, would eventually compulsorily acquire his new site at Heathrow! The airfield was known initially as the 'Harmondsworth Aerodrome' but later as the 'Great West Aerodrome'. It was renowned for its level and smooth turf and the hangar located on the northern corner of the site was said at one time to be the largest in the world. However, this is hard to believe because it was not particularly large.

Because of the obvious advantages, the company decided to expand the site so that it could transfer the factory from Hayes to Heathrow, thus bringing the works and flight testing facilities together. With this end in view Fairey's gradually acquired additional land, as opportunity occurred, and by 1943 they owned about 240 acres of land between Cain's Lane, High Tree Lane and the Duke of Northumberland's River. But for the war, the probabilities are that there would, today, be an aircraft factory at Heathrow with an adjacent aerodrome and the proposed expansion of Heston aerodrome would have gone ahead.

The photographs on pages 11, 12 and 57 clearly show that the presence of the airfield did little to disturb the rural scene: it had no concrete runways, few buildings (at the outbreak of war two additional hangars were provided by the Ministry of Aircraft Production) and only a small number of test flights. The airfield was, in fact, quite a local attraction as it was a novelty then to see aeroplanes at such close quarters.

The Fairey aerodrome and the large numbers of people in the aviation world who visited it at the time of the Royal Aeronautical Society's garden parties were undoubtedly what led the aviation interests to cast covetous eyes on Heathrow as a site for a civil airport for London. However, if war had not broken out in 1939, it would have proved impossible for them to acquire Fairey's airfield and the surrounding land. The war presented the opportunity for the whole area to be requisitioned and to begin the development of a civil airport under the pretext that it was needed as a base for the RAF.

The aerodrome remained in use by Fairey for flight-testing until 1944. From the start the company had hoped that the airfield would be, not only a flight-testing centre, but also a possible site for aircraft assembly, or even a complete new factory. Because of continued difficulties, including official opposition to extending the facilities, the airfield was never properly developed and, as described below, was eventually requisitioned by the Air Ministry in 1944.

The Fairey Airfield in the early 1930s.

Royal Aeronautical Society's garden party, 1935. From 1935 to 1939 the aerodrome was the venue for the garden party of the Royal Aeronautical Society. At these parties a wide variety of aircraft were gathered, from light planes to gliders, from military aircraft to new civil airliners fresh from the production lines. There were also numerous aeronautical displays so that during the one day of the party more people visited Heathrow than the total for the rest of the year. For example, *The Aeroplane* of 8 May 1935 remarked: 'The Garden Party of the Royal Aeronautical Society at Heathrow Aerodrome, Harmondsworth, on 5th May was a success in every way, in entertainment, in atmosphere, in attendance, in setting – and in the weather. Most of the forthcoming season's exhibits have now been displayed in the best possible weather and the most delightful surroundings. The aerodrome, which was kindly lent for the occasion by Mr C.R. Fairey, the Past President of the Society, is certainly one of the finest in the country. Its 'Hunterised' surface stretches away to its distant hedges like a vast green lawn – and it made a perfect setting for frocks and aeroplanes alike. More than 2000 visitors – many of whom arrived by air in the serried rows of Moths which lined the Southern Boundary – had a wonderful afternoon in the sun, rounded off by strawberries and cream in the shade of marquees.'

FLYING PROGRAMME

May 14th, 1939

at

THE FAIREY AVIATION COMPANY'S AERODROME

(The Great West Aerodrome, near Hayes)

(By kind permission of Mr. C. R. Fairey, M.B.E., F.R.Ae.S.)

The following is an outline of the arrangements. They are subject to such alterations as may be found necessary at the time. Any change will be announced on the loud speakers.

‖ It is particularly requested, in order that arrangements may run as smoothly as possible, that ‖ members and their guests will vacate their seats in the marquees as soon as they have had their teas.

p.m.

2.30—3.0 Reception by the President, Mr. A. H. R. Fedden, D.Sc., M.B.E., F.R.Ae.S.
(The reception is at the reception tent near the flagstaff and hangars)

Time	Firm	Pilot	Aircraft	Engine
14.50-14.58	Reid and Sigrist	C. Lowdell	Twin-engined Trainer	2 Gipsy Sixes
15.00-15.08	Vickers Aviation, Ltd.	J. Summers	Wellington	Pegasus XVIII's
15.10-15.18	Blackburn Aircraft, Ltd.	Flt.-Lt. Bailey	Skua	Perseus XII
15.20-15.28	Percival Aircraft, Ltd.	Cpt. Percival	Q.6	2 Gipsy Sixes
		D. M. Bray	Mew Gull	Gipsy VI
15.30-15.38	General Aircraft, Ltd.	D. Hollis-Williams	Cygnet, with tricycle under-carriage	
15.40-15.48	Boulton Paul Aircraft	C. Feather	Defiant	Merlin
15.50-15.58	Fairey Aviation Co.	F. H. Dixon	P4/34	Merlin Rm2M
16.00-16.08	Cierva Autogiro Co.	R. A. C. Brie	Type C40	Salmson 9Nd
16.10-16.38		TEA INTERVAL.		

During the tea interval there will be a demonstration at 16.10-16.24 by 9 Supermarine Spitfires of No. 74 Fighter Squadron, and at 16.26-16.38 a demonstration by 9 Bristol Blenheims of No. 601 Fighter Squadron of the Auxiliary Air Force.

16.40-16.48	The Willoughby Delta Co.	Capt. A. M. Kingwill	Willoughby St. Francis	2 Menasco Pirate C4
		S. Appleby	Schelde Musch	Praga B
16.50-17.18		TEA INTERVAL.		

During the tea interval there will be a demonstration of the following old types of machines:—

	International Horseless Carriage Corporation	R. G. J. Nash	1911 Bleriot XXVII	Gnome
	The Warden Aviation Company	R. O. Shuttleworth	Sopwith Pup	Le Rhone
			Bleriot	
			Deperdussin	Anzani
17.20-17.28	Westland Aircraft, Ltd.	Flt.-Lt. C. N. Snarey	Lysander II	Perseus XII
17.30-17.38	Tipsy Aircraft, Ltd.	Brian Allen		
		A. D. Ward	3 Tipsy's	Walter Mikron
		Capt. J. Youill		
17.40-17.48	Bristol Aeroplane Co.	A. J. Pegg	Bristol Blenheim	Mercury XV's
17.50-17.58	Fairey Aviation Co.	C. S. Staniland	Firefly II	
18.00		A.R.P. Demonstration.		

Flying Programme of the Royal Aeronautical Society 1939. This is the front page of R.Ae.S. programme, giving details of the displays which formed the most popular feature of the Garden Party. It was the last ever public function to take place at the Great West Aerodrome. Within four months war broke out and five years later the airfield was requisitioned by the Air Ministry under the pretext that it was urgently needed as a military airfield.

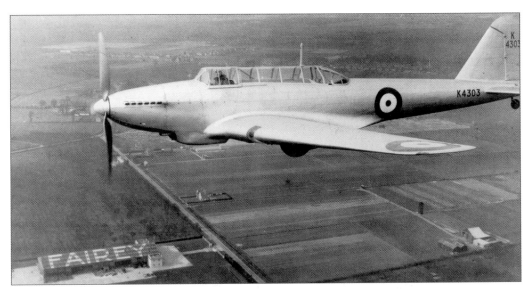

Prototype Fairey Battle bomber flying over the Great West Aerodrome, 1936. Fairey's hangar can be seen immediately under the propeller of the aeroplane. Until the outbreak of war this was the only building on the airfield. The road running diagonally across the foreground of the photograph is Cain's Lane (see also photographs on pages 11, 12 & 58). Photograph by Charles Brown in March 1936, courtesy of RAF Museum, Reference No P 102705.

Model aircraft flying at Heathrow, 1937. Because of his youthful interest in model aeroplanes, Richard Fairey was very sympathetic to the requests of model aeroplane clubs to use his aerodrome at weekends when it was not being used for any other purposes. The aerodrome was the regular Sunday venue for members of the Hayes Model Aeroplane Club who flew their models at Heathrow. It was also used by other clubs which often travelled long distances to use the aerodrome. One of the hazards for the model flying clubs was the Duke of Northumberland's River, which formed the southern boundary of the airfield.

THE SEIZURE OF THE AERODROME BY THE AIR MINISTRY

At the outbreak of war Richard Fairey joined the Ministry of Aircraft Production and in August 1940 he was appointed as deputy to the Air Section of The British Purchasing Commission in Washington. In 1942 he rose to be the Director General of the British Air Mission in which capacity he remained until April 1945. This meant that in the crucial years of 1942–4 Fairey was out of the country at the time that the Air Ministry was planning to requisition his aerodrome at Heathrow. Had he remained in this country, the outcome may well have been different.

Even so it might be thought that, as members of the aviation community, the Fairey Aviation Company would have been given more sympathetic consideration than it in fact received. As the company were manufacturers of military aircraft during wartime, the Ministry of Aircraft Production would not agree to its eviction from the airfield without some alternative arrangement being made for the company's test flights.

Temporary arrangements were therefore reluctantly made for the company to use Heston aerodrome, which was reasonably close to its factory at Hayes. However, this arrangement did not last for long and in 1947, for the third time in its history, the company was evicted yet again by the Air Ministry. It ended up using White Waltham airfield in Berkshire, more than twenty miles away from Hayes.

The effect of the prospective loss of their airfield on the company can be judged from the correspondence that passed between Sir Richard Fairey, the founder of the company, and his co-chairman, Sir Clive Baillieu. When he first learned, officially, of the news on 7 January 1944, Fairey cabled: 'Decision so utterly calamitous, suggest liquidation only practical prospect. However, detailed reply coming quickest route.'

In his detailed reply Fairey wrote:

It is manifestly so much easier for the Civil Aviation authorities to look over the airports near London, that the foresight of private companies has made available, and then using government backing forcibly to acquire them, than to go to the infinite trouble that we had in making an aerial survey to find the site, buying the land from different owners, and then building up a fine airfield from what was market-gardening land. And why the haste to proceed? I cannot escape the thought that the hurry is not uninspired by the fact that a post-war government might not be armed with the power or even be willing to take action that is now being rushed through at the expense of the war effort . . .

My mind concentrates on the fact that it is completely unnecessary for the Civil Aviation authorities to have their airport at Heathrow but it is vital to us. There are hundreds of airports in England. Rapid transport by road and rail to say nothing of helicopter, could easily be made available to them, and within reasonable limits, the further they are from London the better can they operate. The exact reverse applies to us.

Part of the problem facing the company was that the Defence of the Realm Act allowed the Government to requisition land without paying compensation. The dispute dragged on for many years after the war as the Government took a very niggardly approach to the payment of proper compensation to the company. Fairey's claim for the loss of the airfield raised many legal problems and made legal history. Since no legal precedent could be found, the offer was on the basis of the loss of agricultural land. The company countered this by claiming that it was an industrial site and, as such, compensation should be made on this basis. Since the industrial site value was very much greater than that for agricultural use, this claim was rejected by the Government. The legal battle continued until 1964 – twenty years after the airfield had been requisitioned! – when a sum of £1.6 million was finally agreed. By this time Richard Fairey had died (in 1956) but his son was later to say that 'the requisitioning of the aerodrome under wartime powers for civil use was a major scandal which my father never forgave. I very much doubt that he would have agreed to compensation of £1.6 million; the figure could hardly be said to have been generous even in 1964.' (John Fairey – private communication.)

The legal wranglings meant that Fairey's hangar at Heathrow could not be demolished until the question of compensation was settled. The hangar thus survived until 1964 and was the last of the original buildings at Heathrow to be demolished.

Sir Richard Fairey's gloomy prophecies, described above, proved to be well founded and the company was taken over by Westland Helicopters in 1960. Up to this time the company continued to use the White Waltham airfield, but this was a serious handicap: the Heathrow airfield had been only three miles away from the Hayes factory whilst White Waltham was twenty miles distant. Delays and increased maintenance costs in moving aircraft parts (for final assembly and flight-testing) over the increased distance were a daily occurrence. These, over a period of years, must have seriously affected the company's profits and contributed to the take-over by Westland Helicopters.

After the take-over, aircraft continued to be built at the Hayes factory site until it was closed by Westlands in 1972. The site is now an industrial estate the greater part of which was, at first, occupied by Mercedes-Benz and Hitachi. Ironically, these represent the two major powers that Fairey aircraft were employed to fight against in the Second World War – which raises the question of who actually won.

The name of Fairey in the locality has not completely disappeared from Hayes: it lingers on at the junction of North Hyde Road and Station Road, which is still known locally as 'Fairey Corner', and 'Fairey Avenue' is a cul-de-sac off North Hyde Road.

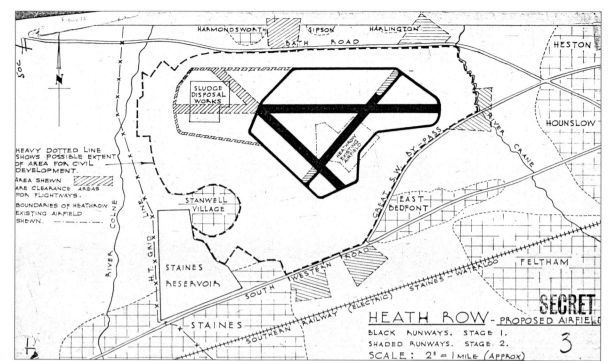

Initial proposals for the airport, 1943. This shows the proposals for the airport finally drawn up in October 1943 and which were submitted to the War Cabinet for approval. The proposals involved the resiting of the Perry Oaks sludge disposal works. The plan shows the runways to be constructed as part of Stage 1 of the development in black. The main east–west runway on the map is further south of the Bath Road than at present, with the sludge works being incorporated into the airport as part of the Stage 2 development. Evidence that the airport was envisaged from the outset as being for civil use can be seen from the boundary showing the possible extent of the area to be taken up for civil development.

CHAPTER SEVEN

WARTIME ORIGINS OF THE AIRPORT

THE ORIGINS OF THE DEVELOPMENT

Although, the Air Ministry was frequently subjected to severe criticism because of its alleged lack of interest in civil aviation matters, there was within the Ministry, unbeknown to its critics, a faction that was fanatically devoted to civil aviation. As events would show, they would go to extraordinary lengths to further its interests and the outbreak of war did nothing to deflect them from their plans, even if it meant diverting valuable resources away from the war effort. This faction was headed by Harold Balfour (of whom more later), the Parliamentary Under Secretary of State for Air who recommended, in a minute dated 23 May 1941, that an Inter-Departmental Committee should be set up to consider Post War Policy For Civil Aviation. 'It may not be too early even now to be thinking which would be suitable aerodromes which have special claims for civil aviation.' (PRO File BT217/2201) This, at a time when Britain stood alone, when it was by no means certain what the outcome of the war would be and when everything was supposed to be subordinated to the war effort.

The idea of constructing a civil airport at Heathrow, rather than at Heston, had been first mooted in 1936, at the time of the acquisition of Heston. But the Air Ministry concluded then that it would be impossible to proceed because of objections from the Fairey Aviation Company (on account of its airfield), the Middlesex County Council (on account of its sludge works) and the Ministry of Agriculture. The outbreak of war presented the Air Ministry with the opportunity to acquire the land compulsorily under the pretext that it was required as an airfield by the RAF.

Although many thought at the time that the primary, if not the only purpose, of the development of the airport was for civil aviation, the pretence that it was developed in response to the urgent need for a military airfield close to London is still officially maintained; even now most accounts give this as the reason for the development. It was not until 1973, in the autobiography of Harold Balfour (later Lord Balfour of Inchrye), that the truth was finally admitted. Balfour, the Parliamentary Under Secretary of State for Air between 1938 and 1944, made the astonishing claim in *Wings Over Westminster* (1973):

Almost the last thing I did in the Air Ministry of any importance was to hi-jack for Civil Aviation the land on which London Airport stands under the noses of resistant Ministerial colleagues. If hi-jack is too strong a term I plead guilty to the lesser crime of deceiving a cabinet Committee. Within the Department those of us who had studied post-war civil aviation needs knew that spreading out from the Fairey Aviation Company's small grass aerodrome on the Great West Staines Road was land ideal for

London's main airport. We also knew that any thought of trying to get the land for civil aviation would have to go through complicated civil procedures and was bound to be resisted by Agriculture and Housing and maybe more Ministries. Therefore our only hope lay in taking over the Fairey field and adjacent land under wartime powers and regulations. These powers were drastic and positive and should not be employed for anything but war purposes. I advanced as powerfully as I could the case for the need. I did not dare to breathe the words 'Civil Aviation'. I put this right out of my mind so effectively that I really convinced myself of the priority of our case. The Cabinet came down on our side.

Balfour's account seems so improbable that at the time it was given little credence, being seen merely as the idle boasts of a vain old man who had completely lost the wit to distinguish fact from fantasy and right from wrong. Another of his boasts was that, as a fighter pilot in the First World War war, he shot at his victims when they attempted to parachute to safety. Even a major war criminal, such as Hermann Goering, was appalled by this practice and he instructed his Luftwaffe pilots that they were not to murder their opponents in this manner.

The account certainly does not correspond with the account given by Douglas Jay in his autobiography (*Change and Fortune*, 1980) in which he recorded: 'In my last months with the Ministry of Supply, I was asked to attend a meeting at the Air Ministry to decide on a site for a post-war civil airport . . . about six of us assembled at Assistant Secretary level. The meeting lasted forty minutes and we decided on Heathrow.' The file in the Public Record Office (BT217/441) shows that Jay's account is incorrect and that he was referring to a meeting which he attended on 7 March 1945, when the construction, ostensibly as a military airfield, was well under way.

This much is known from the files, now in the PRO, which make it abundantly clear that Balfour's account is substantially correct except in one important respect. The significant, if perhaps not surprising (given his odd sense of values), omission in Balfour's account is that he was not the prime instigator. In fact, the origin of Heathrow came from S.A. Dismore, who, pre-war, had been Assistant General Manager of Imperial Airways (which became BOAC in 1939). At the outbreak of war he joined the RAF and in December 1942 he wrote an internal memorandum, stating the alleged need for a new major airport for air transport operations in the London area and stating that Heston was probably the most suitable answer 'but Heathrow is also a possibility'. With his background it is obvious that he had in mind an airport for civil use, and in fact it was the BOAC that was the instigator of the original plans. In early 1943, it made a survey of the area and came up with proposals for a civil airport at Heathrow which it presented to the Air Ministry.

The Ministry was a very willing partner but, realising that it could not possibly acquire the land for the development of a civil airfield, it had to resort to the pretext that the land was needed for a military airfield so that it could be compulsorily requisitioned under the terms of the Defence of the Realm Act. The Ministry therefore drew up its own proposals in August 1943 for the development of an airport at Heathrow which are shown on page 62.

The plan did not correspond with the wishes of BOAC and according to an Air Ministry internal minute:

There has been a good deal of complaint with Heathrow from BOAC which has put forward alternative proposals for the development of the site . . . the Corporation has not ceased to complain that full weight is not being given to its views. But as the present plan is a purely military project, this plan has not been discussed with the Corporation. Indeed since Fairey's are being displaced under wartime powers, much against their will, it is most important, until the civil scheme is approved by Government, to preserve the position that the present plan is a purely military one not open to criticism by BOAC. (PRO File BT217/441)

Even when the ministry had completed its plans it was still worried about the reaction of the War Cabinet to its proposals as can be seen from a minute, dated 11 October 1943, sent to Balfour by G.C. Pirie the Director General of Operations. In this he says:

The weakness of our argument will remain as long as we try to justify the construction of Heathrow on military grounds. It is most desirable to prove conclusively that we do require an airfield for military purposes on the Heathrow site and that no existing airfield could satisfactorily be adapted for this purpose at less cost and disturbance. My own view is that the argument on military grounds is patently weak, and the most we can hope for is that the Cabinet will fully appreciate the post-war civil aviation aspect and reluctantly agree that the military case is just good enough to justify the means to an end. (PRO File AIR 19/388)

Although to begin with, the Air Ministry was happy for BOAC to be represented at the Heathrow development meetings, it became increasingly alarmed that BOAC's grandiose plans might divulge the real reason for the development. The Ministry therefore excluded the Corporation from the meetings which led to increasing friction between the two parties.

However, this did not stop the complaints and BOAC caused consternation when an article, obviously inspired by the Corporation, appeared in the *Daily Mail* on 14 March 1944 which was headlined 'London May Get Biggest Airport'. This reported the Director General of BOAC, A.C. Critchley, as saying that 'the planning of post-war air services cannot go ahead properly until my corporation is given a permanent home'. He then went on to reveal that he had Heathrow in mind by talking about a site only thirteen miles from Hyde Park Corner. In a companion article, which appeared in *The Aeroplane* on 24 March, Critchley was quoted as saying that '*BOAC had selected an ideal site* [author's emphasis] for an airport but had failed to persuade the Government to come to a decision.'

Fortunately for the Ministry, the article did not have much impact, probably because Crichley had clearly entered the realms of fantasy when he went on to talk of also having a water strip parallel to the main runway on which seaplanes could land!

The proposals for development envisaged construction in three stages, and at a meeting on 12 November 1943 the War Cabinet provisionally accepted this recommendation (PRO File AVIA 2/2269). This opened the way for the development to begin but there were still several difficulties to be overcome, including worries about the legality of the action being taken. On this point, advice was sought from the Treasury Solicitor in a minute dated 4 February 1944 which gives the information that 'On the matter generally you should be aware that the ultimate object is to provide a suitable (civil) airport for London. Were there no other object it would be a question of Civil Aviation only and presumably Defence Regulations could not have been used for obtaining provision of land for use for normal peace-time purposes.' (PRO File AVIA 2/2274)

The Treasury Solicitor was particularly concerned about the requisitioning of the Perry Oaks sludge works (which is discussed later). He advised that, if the War Cabinet approved the scheme, it was imperative to avoid any public statements that linked the development with any post-war use of the airfield for civil aviation. He suggested that if the Ministry were challenged in Parliament or elsewhere about the propriety of the use of the Defence of the Realm Act for requisitioning the land at Heathrow, it should use the following statement to justify its actions:

It is essential for war purposes to requisition and to do all that we propose to do now at Heathrow. When the war purposes end we shall have to consider whether we are going to carry out our statutory obligations to reinstate and return the land or whether we are going to seek Parliamentary powers, either general or specific to deal otherwise with the land, assuming that powers have not meanwhile been made available. (PRO File AIR 19/388)

The exchanges with the Treasury Solicitor leave no doubt of the true intentions of those concerned within the Air Ministry, who pursued their aim with zeal even though it meant diverting valuable resources away from the war effort at a time when the preparations for the Normandy landings were well under way.

INHIBITING FACTORS

Two factors inhibited the Air Ministry's proposals: one was the presence of the sludge disposal works at Perry Oaks; the other was the attitude of Winston Churchill. Other factors which might have been thought to have played a part, such as the problem of aircraft noise, the fate of the inhabitants who were to be evicted from their homes and the effects on the Fairey Aviation Company and on agriculture, were completely ignored. The effects of the development of the airport on Fairey's and on the important West Middlesex market gardening industry have already been considered earlier. The remaining factors are considered in this section.

NOISE

In view of the major problems caused by aircraft noise it is quite extraordinary that there is no mention of noise anywhere in the files and the problem seems to have been entirely ignored. Colin Buchanan in *No Way To The Airport* (1981) has commented on this strange omission and one can do no better than to quote him on this:

There were so many unbelievably noisy aircraft around in 1944 that it seems incredible that a so potent side-effect of aviation could have been overlooked. But overlooked it was. Heathrow was developed with a pair of parallel runways running due east-west pointing in one direction at point-blank range straight into the huge housing mass of West London and in the other direction, straight at Windsor only six miles away – Windsor of all places, historic town, royal residence, famous schools, glorious stretch of river, parks and gardens beyond compare. Heathrow is fifteen miles from the middle of London. This comparatively close proximity to the heart of a big city has presumably paid dividends over the years in respect of reduced travelling time to and from the airport, but the misery which the flight paths have spread, also over many years, far and wide over a huge part of London and the Home Counties, must surely make that decision in 1943 the most disastrous planning disaster to hit our country.

In this disaster area live half a million people, whose daily lives are constantly disrupted by aircraft noise. The very layout of Heathrow is an affront to the rights and well-being of those who live under the airport's flight paths. 'Tolerate or emigrate' are not options for these people or places. Here are Windsor Castle, Hampton Court, Chiswick House, Kew Gardens, Richmond Park, Syon Park and Osterley Park, all historic and attractive places severely disturbed by overflying aircraft.

Low flying aircraft over Kew Gardens, 1998. Depending on wind direction and on which runway is in use, Kew Gardens along with Windsor Castle, Richmond Park, Osterley Park, Syon Park and other sites of immense amenity value, are subjected to low-flying aircraft passing overhead at intervals of little more than one minute.

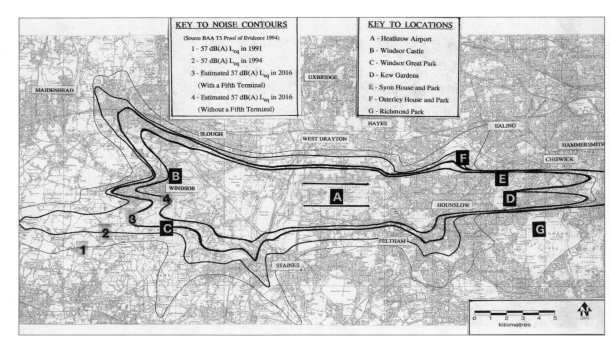

KEY TO NOISE CONTOURS

(Source BAA T5 Proof of Evidence 1994)

1 - 57 dB(A) L$_{eq}$ in 1991

2 - 57 dB(A) L$_{eq}$ in 1994

3 - Estimated 57 dB(A) L$_{eq}$ in 2016
(With a Fifth Terminal)

4 - Estimated 57 dB(A) L$_{eq}$ in 2016
(Without a Fifth Terminal)

KEY TO LOCATIONS

A - Heathrow Airport

B - Windsor Castle

C - Windsor Great Park

D - Kew Gardens

E - Syon House and Park

F - Osterley House and Park

G - Richmond Park

57 dB(A) Leq noise contour around Heathrow in relation to areas of high amenity value. Contours of noise exposure can be mapped out around an airport in a similar manner to the contour lines used on maps to signify differences in height. Noise annoyance is defined by the 'Equivalent Continuous Sound Level' (Leq) with 57 Leq being considered as being the onset of annoyance. For those living close to the airport the situation is of course much worse and the Inspector reporting on the 4th Terminal Inquiry concluded that 'In my view the present levels of noise around Heathrow are unacceptable in a civilised society.' The map shows the area affected by daytime noise in 1991, and as predicted for 2016 with and without a fifth terminal. This is a considerable improvement on the position 10 years earlier because of the introduction of less noisy aircraft. BAA claims that it will improve still more because of the introduction of what it euphemistically calls 'quieter' aircraft, even with the construction of a fifth terminal and the extra traffic that this would bring. However, even BAA has to admit that some of these improvements would be negated if a fifth terminal were to be built. On its own figures, 560,800 people were adversely affected by aircraft noise in 1991. This would drop by 59 per cent to 231,800 by 2016 if a fifth terminal were not built, but only by 35 per cent to 363,400 with a fifth terminal.

THE FATE OF THE INHABITANTS

The welfare of the people to be evicted to make way for the airport received scant consideration from the authorities. Many of them came from families who had lived in the Heathrow area for generations, but they were treated worse than if they had been refugees from a foreign country. The Air Ministry was, indeed, loath to accept any responsibility for them at all and tried to get the Ministry of Health (then responsible for housing) and the local authorities to find alternative accommodation, at a time when these bodies were desperately engaged on re-housing people whose houses had been destroyed by the V1 attacks on London. Faced with the refusal of these organisations to help, the Ministry even considered the possibility of forcibly billeting the unfortunate people in other houses in the area with all the problems that would have entailed. In the end, the Ministry used accommodation already in its possession or in the possession of other service Ministries, and most refugees from the Stage 1 development were re-housed at Heston in property adjoining the aerodrome. (PRO File AVIA 2/2271 and personal knowledge)

In the case of landowners, their property was requisitioned, but not purchased, as the Defence Regulations envisaged that in many cases the requisitioned property would be returned to its original owners after the war. The owners were therefore paid a compensation rental by the Government on the supposition that they had let their land and property to the authorities for the duration of the war. In the case of Heathrow it appears that there was never any intention of returning the land to its rightful owners, but the pretence was made that it might be. Consequently, the landowners did not receive proper compensation until well after the war and even then only at pre-war values.

Apart from this, the terms of compensation were extremely harsh. One farmer, before he left, took away his greenhouses and sheds; the value of these was deducted from his eventual compensation even to the extent that the value of his front gate and hedge, which he also removed, was taken into account. Had he left them in place they would have been destroyed, as they were of no value to the Air Ministry.

The same attitude was adopted in awarding compensation for growing crops, which were regularly inspected by the Air Ministry before the owners were evicted. In one case a deduction was made, 'because the crop (of broad beans) was seriously affected by black fly . . . and my notes show that the crop of lettuce had not been watered'. As if a farmer would regularly spray his beans and water his lettuce when he knew full well that they were likely to be destroyed before they reached maturity!

Demolitions in connexion with the airport development, 1944. Winnie Baker, a Land Girl, standing by a partially demolished farm building in Cain's Lane. It had originally been a Methodist Chapel but had been unused for this purpose since 1870. In the centre background are four farm cottages and to their left is Palmer's Farm.

Temple Bar 5411
XXXHOLBORN 3434.

TELEPHONE:
Extn. 9236

Any communications on the subject of this letter should be addressed to :—

THE UNDER SECRETARY OF STATE, AIR MINISTRY, and the following number quoted :—

A.632131/44/W.6.b.3./R.88

Your Ref.

AIR MINISTRY,

LONDON, W.C.2.

2nd May
~~February~~, 1944.

Sir,

Property at Heath Row.

I am directed to inform you that the airfield at Heath Row is to be enlarged in the near future and it will be necessary for this purpose to take over your property possession of which, it is anticipated, will be required not later than 24·7·1944. Formal Notice of Requisition, in duplicate, is enclosed, one copy of which should be signed and returned in the accompanying franked envelope.

Three copies of Claim Form 1, in respect of your interest as occupier, are also enclosed which, on completion, should be returned, in duplicate, to the Air Ministry. In this connection, it is pointed out that under Section 11 of the Compensation (Defence) Act, 1939, your claim must be lodged within six months from the date on which the compensation accrues due, that is, the date on which possession is taken, as otherwise it will not be entertained.

Before any work is done on the property a Lands Officer will visit the site and discuss with you detailed arrangements for taking possession. Subject to essential Air Ministry requirements, every facility will be given to enable you to remove your movable property and effects and any growing crops.

The property is being taken over under the Defence Regulations but this will not preclude sale and purchase by agreement if the Air Ministry decides that it is required for permanent retention.

In conclusion, I am to draw attention to the fact that the Defence Regulations prohibit the making of any sketch, plan or other representation of any prohibited place. This prohibition applies to the making of any sketch or plan of R.A.F. Stations or defence works, etc., or the marking on any such sketch or plan of any Stations or works.

I am, Sir,
Your obedient Servant,

Notice of eviction May, 1944. The first official intimation of possible eviction of the local residents was the receipt of a letter from the Air Ministry in May 1943. This was followed by the letter reproduced here, giving notice to quit, which was clearly intended to be sent in February 1944, but was not in fact posted until 2 May 1944. The delay in sending the second letter was undoubtedly due to the receipt on 12 February of Churchill's minute to the Air Ministry, referred to later, which led to a delay in final approval until 13 April.

THE PERRY OAKS PROBLEM

The presence of the sludge works at Perry Oaks posed enormous problems. At a meeting of the Airport Committee on 27 January 1944 it was decided that it would only be possible to proceed if the Air Ministry could satisfy the War Cabinet that the sludge works could be removed within two years because, as the minutes recorded: 'Clearly we shall run the risk of serious criticism if we do not complete Stages 1 and 2 of the construction before the end of the Japanese war. The task must be to persuade the Middlesex County Council to undertake the removal of their Sludge Works in such time that we shall be able to complete Stages 1 and 2 within the two-year period.' (PRO File AIR 19/388)

The Defence of the Realm Act 1939 which was used to acquire the land for development, allowed the authorities to requisition at short notice land deemed to be needed in connexion with the pursuit of the war without any right of appeal. In theory the sludge works could therefore have been acquired under the Act but this presented major problems and the Treasury Solicitor advised against it. The problems centred around the practical difficulty that the works could not just be closed down: another site would have to be found. In the Solicitor's opinion:

> It was a tall order to use Defence powers to plant a sludge works in somebody's back garden without giving the injured party the opportunity of being heard. When wartime buildings were put up on private land under compulsory powers the broad assumption was that, at the end of the war, the buildings would be removed and the amenities restored. But a sludge works was a different proposition; it was essentially permanent in character. While Defence powers could properly be used by the Secretary of State for Air to take possession of the land it would be a gross abuse of these powers unless we were satisfied that there was no practical alternative. (PRO File AIR 19/388)

These developments were unwelcome news to the Ministry and long and ill-tempered negotiations were held with the Middlesex County Council, which owned the works. The Council was, in fact, trying to be helpful but it could see no possibility of finding an alternative site without resort to a public inquiry. This the Air Ministry was determined to avoid at all costs as an inquiry would have revealed the true reasons behind the acquisition of the land. Rather than face a public inquiry the Air Ministry revised the layout of the airport which avoided taking the works in the first instance. The failure to secure the sludge works was a major blow to the Ministry which recognised that the amended plan 'would give an aerodrome that might not meet Civil Aviation requirements after the war . . . it would leave the post-war Government to face the problem of the removal of the sludge works, with all its attendant political difficulties'. (PRO File AIR 19/388) This, of course, has proved to be more true than the writer could have ever possibly imagined!

THE ATTITUDE OF WINSTON CHURCHILL

Although the problems of noise and the fate of the unfortunate inhabitants of Heathrow who faced eviction from their homes never even entered the minds of the Air Ministry officials, a problem that could not be ignored was a minute from the Prime Minister himself, addressed to the Secretary of State for Air (Sir Archibald Sinclair), dated 12 February 1944. In this

Churchill stated: 'We ought not to withdraw 3,000 men for this purpose (the development of the airport) until OVERLORD is over. . . . OVERLORD dominates the scene. I shall suggest to the Cabinet that the project be reconsidered in six months time . . .' (OVERLORD was the code name for the Normandy landings.) (PRO File AIR 19/388)

Churchill's minute caused consternation in the Air Ministry, which foresaw that if the project were to be delayed for six months from the Normandy landing, the war in Europe could well be over and the reasons given for the development of Heathrow would disappear. Making a virtue of necessity, the Air Ministry therefore put forward the revised plan which avoided the Perry Oaks sludge works and Sinclair, in a further minute to Churchill, informed him that 'A new scheme has been prepared, the essence of which is that by re-siting runways it enables us to meet war needs more quickly and with much less manpower during the OVERLORD period.'

Sinclair failed to reveal that the modified proposals meant, as the Air Ministry well knew, that if they eventually gained subsequent approval for the development of a civil airport, one of the runways proposed in the revised plan would have to be demolished. This fact is clear from the reaction of BOAC which, although it had been excluded from the discussions, continued to snipe at the Ministry from the sidelines and repeatedly complained about the unsuitability of the revised proposals for its civil aviation requirements.

In the early part of 1944 Churchill obviously had far more important things to worry about than the development of Heathrow and no doubt this was the reason why he eventually gave his reluctant consent. Following this, approval for the development was given at the meeting of the War Cabinet held on 13 April 1944. The Civil Aviation lobby in the Air Ministry had won and development started in June, the month of the Normandy landings and of the first V-1 attacks on London. It shows their determination to push ahead at all costs with the project, even if it meant diverting valuable resources away from the war effort.

Heathrow Airport under construction, 1945. View from the south-west with the Perry Oaks sludge works in the foreground. The runway, going diagonally across the photograph, had to be built to keep up the pretence that the airport was needed by the RAF. Its construction was opposed by BOAC because it was entirely unsuitable for civil aviation and it was subsequently abandoned. The writer of a minute, dated 9 January 1946, later made rueful reference to this fact when he said: 'The NW/SE runway constructed by the RAF is completely redundant. That this runway might eventually be redundant to the civil scheme was known when construction commenced, but the period of use of the redundant runway will be less than two years. Its cost will have been approx £350,000' [at 1946 prices]. (PRO File AIR 19/388) (*Photograph courtesy of the RAF Museum, Reference No. 6082-9*)

Heathrow Airport under construction, 1946. This photograph, which was taken on 7 June 1946, is roughly divided in two by the Bath Road (A4) which runs across the photograph from WSW to ENE. North of the Bath Road are the villages of Sipson on the left and Harlington on the right, both destined at that time to be demolished for the extension of the airport. The northern runway has been completed and between it and the Bath Road, in the middle of the photograph, is what was then the terminal area with three aeroplanes on the ground. Further south the devastation continues but vestiges of Cain's Lane and Heathrow Road still survive.

CHAPTER EIGHT

DEVELOPMENT OF THE AIRPORT, 1944–60

The Air Ministry's original proposals were to construct the airport in three stages. Stage 1 and 2 are shown in the map on page 62. The difficulty of finding an alternative site for the Perry Oaks sludge works without holding a public inquiry led to these proposals being abandoned.

Stage 3 was put forward at the first meeting held, on 10 August 1943, of the Departmental Committee which had been set up to consider the development of Heathrow. At that meeting a completely new plan for the development was proposed. It involved moving the site to the north and centring it on the Bath Road. However, it was considered that, although this scheme had considerable merits, 'no Government would be prepared to consider a project that involved razing the three old-world villages of Harmondsworth, Sipson and Harlington to the ground' (PRO File AVIA 2/2270) and the matter of a possible Stage 3 development was not pursued at that time. This rebuff did not put an end to the proposal and characteristically the Air Ministry continued to make plans which involved the extension of the airport north of the Bath Road. The possibility was later raised again and, as will be seen later, eventually gained approval.

The modified Stage 1 had not been completed when the airport was transferred from the Air Ministry to the Ministry of Civil Aviation (MCA) on 1 January 1946. Despite all the spurious claims about the urgent RAF need, the airport had never been used by the RAF and the first use of the airport was for a civil flight, which took place for publicity purposes, when a British South American Airways Lancastrian took off on a long-distance proving flight to South America. The airport was formally opened on 31 May 1946.

Aircraft on the runway at Heathrow, 1946. In the foreground is a Lancaster bomber, the type of aircraft for which the airport was supposed to have been built in pursuit of the war effort. In the background is a Lancastrian (derived from the Lancaster) civil airliner, which exemplifies the type of aircraft for which the airport was always intended from the very beginning.

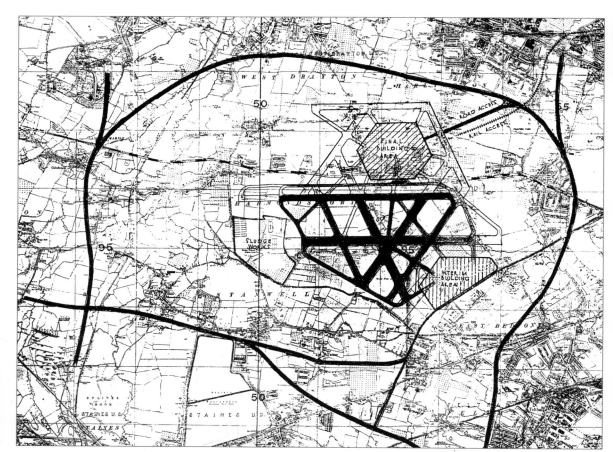

Proposals for the extended airport, 1945. This is one of a number of plans drawn up by the Air Ministry for the extension of the airport. The area of the airport south of the Bath Road as it was at that time is depicted in black. It involved moving the centre of the airport to the north of the Bath Road, which would have been closed. It was to be replaced by a ring road, the northern and western parts of which closely follow the routes of the M4 and M25 – the civil aviation lobby is nothing if not far-sighted and it never gives up! The plan also shows a rail link between the main line at Hayes and the centre of the airport. It was to be another fifty years before the airport had such a link.

Before the transfer of the airport to the MCA, a Cabinet Committee on Civil Aviation had been set up. This Committee recommended that the name of the airport should be changed from 'Heathrow' to 'London Airport' on the grounds that 'Heathrow' was difficult for most foreigners to pronounce (the Committee rejected the fatuous recommendation made earlier that the airport should be renamed 'St George's Airport'). The Committee also revised the proposed stages of development: three stages were still envisaged but these differed considerably from the previous proposals (PRO File BT 217/237). The stages now planned were as follows:

Stage 1
This was to be completed by 31 December 1947 and involved the compulsory purchase of all the land required for the airport south of the Bath Road. This meant the acquisition of 2,650 acres of land, including the 1,590 acres requisitioned by the RAF under the Defence of the Realm Act, and the demolition of 215 houses.

Stage 2.
This was to be completed by 31 December 1949 and did not involve any further acquisition of land or buildings.

Stage 3
This was to be completed in the period 1950–53 and involved the resurrection of the proposals to extend the airport north of the Bath Road. It included the purchase of 1600 acres of land and the re-housing of the occupants of 950 houses (for presentational reasons the Committee decided to refer to the number of houses rather than the number of people, which was in excess of 3,000).

When Stage 3 was announced in 1946 no firm dates were given as to when the extension of the airport to the north of the Bath Road would take place. By 1948 serious delays were occurring with the development of the airport and concern was being expressed about the costs. The date of the extensions was therefore deferred to 1955 at the earliest. Uncertainty as to when or whether the airport would be extended continued with the Ministry of Civil Aviation's cat-and-mouse policy of threatening to come north of the Bath Road but refusing to say when, other than that it would not be before 1955. By mid-1952, however, doubts were beginning to be expressed as to whether the airport would ever be extended across to the north side of the Bath Road, although as late as 20 November 1952 the Ministry was still maintaining that the airport would eventually be extended. However, this was obviously bravado, since less than three weeks later on 10 December the Minister for Civil Aviation announced in Parliament that 'the additional amount of traffic which could be accepted by extending the Airport north of the Bath Road would not justify the expenditure and disturbance incurred'. Thus reprieved from the death sentence, the villages around the airport were instead sentenced to life imprisonment, with the airport as their neighbour. Forty years later the life sentence was re-considered and they were again recommended to be put to death.

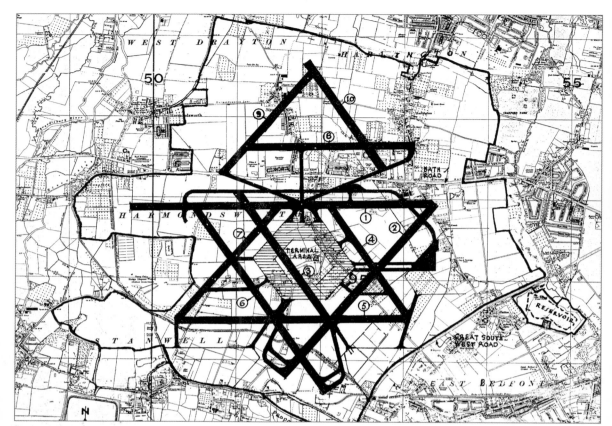

Proposals for the extended airport, 1946. The Stage 3 proposals to extend the airport north of the Bath Road were agreed by the Cabinet on 10 January 1946 (PRO File AIR 19/388). They involved the complete destruction of Sipson and the greater part of Harlington. The map shows that the proposed northern boundary approximately follows the line of the M4 motorway, conceived in 1946 as a replacement for the Bath Road, which would have had to be closed.

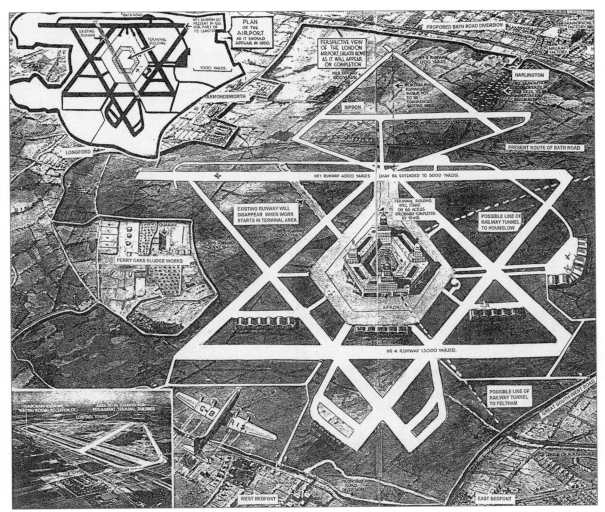

Artist's impression of the extended airport, 1946. This drawing, based on the plan shown on the previous page, appeared in the *Illustrated London News*. It shows two rail links to the airport: one to the London Underground from Hounslow, and one to the Southern Region mainline at Feltham. The underground link did not materialise until 1976 and a link to a mainline station (Paddington not Feltham) did not open until 1998.

Aerial view of Sipson, *c*. 1948. This photograph was taken in connexion with the proposal to extend the airport north of the Bath Road. One of the proposals was to develop an area for helicopter landings between Sipson and Harlington. Although the proposed extension of the airport was abandoned in 1952, airport-related activities have crept northwards so that the pleasant rural scene depicted in the photograph has been destroyed.

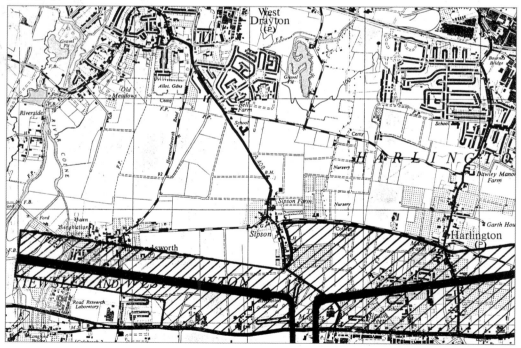

Modified proposals for the extended airport, 1950. In October 1950 the Ministry of Civil Aviation announced that it had revised its plans for the airport extension. The revised plan involved a smaller area of land and reprieved parts of Harlington and Sipson. However, Harmondsworth, which hitherto had been just outside the threatened area, now found itself a potential victim.

Bentalls Values are on page 7

Middlesex Advertiser and

BUCKINGHAMSHIRE ADVERTISER
B   THE UXBRIDGE GAZETTE
ESTABLISHED IN 1840 AS "BROADWATER'S JOURNAL"
The Old-Established

Vol. CX. No. 5856   FRIDAY, DECEMBER 19,

In the slipstream of the Airport news : thousands rejoice and give thanks

'THE MOST WONDERFUL CHRISTMAS BOX WE'VE EVER HAD'

MORE LIGHT BUT—

He is not very partial to gas

COUNCILLOR ROUGH does not like gas — not the kind in evidence at council meetings, but the kind used for street lighting ... and West

REJOICING and thanksgiving, following the news in last week's Advertiser-Gazette that London Airport will not be extended north of the Bath-road, has been in evidence this week all over the affected area.

A psychological "dead hand" has been lifted. Dozens of people interviewed all made the same general comment — "It's the most wonderful Christmas present we've ever had."

For years many thousands of people, firms, and or-

Front page of the *Middlesex Advertiser and Gazette*, 19 December 1952. Locally the news that the airport was not to be extended north of the Bath Road was greeted with delight. The futility of the years of uncertainty was well summed up in the editorial:

> For over six years there has been an intermittent controversy regarding the effect of London Airport plans on the communities settled in the land to be occupied. Every now and then there would be a 'final' revision of the plan to add impetus to the controversy. The Government's decision last week (to abandon the plan) makes it plain that the grandiose scheme for the airport as first planned was adopted too easily without due regard to the consequences to the people it was proposed to disturb. Now that the part of the plan for the northern side of the Bath Road has been found to be not needed, all the anxiety and loss which has been the lot of the inhabitants of the threatened area over the past six years is shown to have been unnecessary and it could have been avoided if there had been more consideration and earlier consultation with the people concerned.

The same editorial also had some harsh things to say about public apathy and the lack of support for the resistance groups formed to fight the extension of the airport. Some of these groups, now transformed into residents' and amenity associations, survive and like to think that they were responsible for preventing the development. In fact as the editorial goes on to say:

> The case for the inhabitants (and those concerned are in an area far larger than the actual site proposed for the airport) has had far too feeble support from the public. There have been a few valiant fighters but they have lacked the strong public backing sufficient to impress the authorities. The few have stuck to their guns but it would be a mistake to assume that the Government has capitulated to their protestations. The reason for the Government's decision is that the extension of the Airport is no longer considered necessary, and that is something entirely different.

Control Tower, Heathrow, *c.* 1946. An airport cannot operate without a control tower so this was one of the first buildings to be erected. It was a crude utilitarian building with direct access from the Bath Road just a short distance to the north. It stood roughly where the airport police station now stands.

Terminal area, 1946. The first 'terminal' area was this temporary tented accommodation hastily erected on the north side of the airport. There was no clear need for the airport to be brought into use so hastily and, until such time as the airport was ready, flights could easily have been made from one of the RAF bases close to London. Indeed RAF Northolt was used by British European Airways for civil flights until 1954. There were others reasonably close to London which would have had much better facilities for passengers and caused them far less inconvenience. However, this would have raised the question as to why one of these bases had not been developed in preference to Heathrow. (*Photograph courtesy of BAA plc*)

Terminal area, 1946. Another view of the tented terminal area, taken from the Bath Road. In the foreground is the signboard of what was then the Bricklayer's Arms (see below).

The Air Hostess. This public house began life as the Bricklayer's Arms. It replaced a pub of the same name which was demolished in 1928 to allow for the widening of the Bath Road. It stood directly opposite the temporary terminal area (see above) and was re-named in 1954. It was demolished in 1988 and its site is now occupied by a drive-in McDonalds.

'Departure Lounge', and Flight Departure, 1946. These photographs clearly show the primitive facilities that were available to passengers and the inconvenience to which they were put so as to keep up the pretence that there was an urgent need for an airfield at Heathrow. The top photograph shows the interior of one of the tents depicted in the previous photograph; the lower photograph shows the absurdity of expecting passengers to put up with such conditions merely to maintain the elaborate pretence. (*Photographs courtesy of BAA plc*)

Terminal buildings, late 1940s. The tents shown in the earlier photographs soon gave way to these pre-fabricated buildings which continued in use until the central terminal area was developed.

Exterior of terminal area, 1951. The facilities offered to passengers in the temporary terminal buildings were so primitive that they came to the attention of the local Public Health inspectors. This photograph is one of a series showing the disgusting conditions discovered by the PHIs which were used as evidence to bring a prosecution against the airport authorities. A close examination of the area in front of the two oil drums towards the rear reveals the presence of a dead rat! The pair of cottages in the background were situated on the other side of the Bath Road just to the east of its junction with Bolton's Lane.

Access tunnel to the central terminal area. *Top*, 1955; *bottom, c.* 1985. The tunnel was constructed initially to provide access from the Bath Road to the central terminal area. It opened to traffic in 1953 and in 1965 a spur road was opened between the M4 motorway and the entrance to the tunnel. The tunnel originally had two lanes for traffic with provision for pedestrians at a higher level in the remaining lane on each side. The pedestrian access lanes have since been converted for use by traffic.

Visitors' area, early 1950s. By the early 1950s a visitors' enclosure had been installed where plane-spotters could watch the aircraft taking off and also go on short pleasure flights.

No. 1 Building Europa (Terminal 2), *c.* 1956. This terminal opened as the Europa building for use by both British and European airlines in 1955. It was the first terminal to open at Heathrow and was re-named Terminal 2 after Terminal 1 was opened in 1968.

No. 2 Building Britannic, *c.* 1956. This is an extension of the Europa building which can be seen on the extreme left. It was initially used for domestic flights (hence the name) and now forms part of Terminal 2.

Queen's Building, *c.* 1956. This was the third major building in the Central Terminal area. It is used as the pilots' administration and briefing centre where aircrews report and receive flight plans. As can be seen from the number of people on the roof, it contains an observation area which was a replacement for the visitors' enclosure seen in the photograph on page 87. Originally the building also contained public restaurants and a news cinema. On the extreme right the clock of what was then the Europa building can just be seen.

Central Terminal area. Above, late 1950s. In the centre is the Queen's Building with what is now Terminal 2 to the left. Work has just begun on the site of Terminal 1 on the right. Below, early 1960s. The control tower and the rear of what is now Terminal 2.

No 3. Passenger Building (Terminal 3), *c.* 1962. This terminal, also known as the 'Oceanic Building', opened for long-haul flights in 1962. In 1968 it was re-named Terminal 3 and extensively re-developed. The lower photograph shows the departure lounge before the terminal was brought into use. Since then shops have taken over much of the floor area of all the terminals, so passengers no longer have the luxury of so much seating space.

Terminal 1, 1974. Despite its name this terminal was the last of the three to be built in the central terminal area. It was opened in November 1968 and became fully operational in May 1969.

Plane crash, 1963. In its fifty years of existence the airport has had a remarkable safety record. The worst accident was in 1972 when a Trident crashed soon after take-off, killing all 118 people on board. Several less serious accidents have occurred, including that shown here. The local paper for 14 November 1963 reported that 'the DC 8 jet (shown in the photograph) failed to take off and carried on a further 700 yards from the end of the runway to come to rest in a field of cabbages. Nobody was seriously injured but a few extra seconds and the plane would have ploughed into Longford Village.'

CHAPTER NINE

FROM COACHING INNS
TO AIRPORT HOTELS

When the airport was first built, the Bath Road (A4) was the only means of gaining access to the airport from London. And although the M4 motorway and rail links have since been built, it still remains an important route to the airport. This is particularly true in the case of the many hotels which now occupy the Bath Road frontage along the northern perimeter of the airport.

Two hundred years ago the Bath Road was the most important route to Bath and Bristol which was then the leading provincial city in England and the major port of departure for the Americas. By the standards of the time the road was one of the busiest in the country as, before the advent of the railway, it was the only means of travelling from London to Bristol. The traffic reached its peak in 1830 when every day there were some fifty stage-coaches and four mail coaches passing along the road in each direction, in addition to a considerable amount of more local traffic.

The frequency of the stage-coaches on the Bath Road and the loneliness of the adjoining heathland attracted highwaymen to the area and Hounslow Heath was notorious for their presence in the mid-eighteenth century. Dick Turpin is often claimed to be associated with the area but there is no evidence that he ever operated on the Bath Road. Many of the remaining coaching inns claim a spurious association with him, but his main area of activity was the Great North Road. Nor is it clear why anybody should regard these so-called 'Gentlemen of the Highway' as anything other than ruffians who richly deserved the sentences that they received when they were caught. Two hundred years later, in the 1960s, the airport was to earn the nickname 'Thiefrow' (its companion airport was 'Snatchquick') on account of its baggage handlers who seemed to think that pilfering of passengers' baggage was one of the perquisites of their job. On one occasion, they threatened to go on strike when some of their number were charged with theft!

To cater for the travellers on the road, a large number of coaching inns were built in much the same way as airport hotels have now appeared. In fact, in the vicinity of Heathrow, many of the old coaching inns have since disappeared to make way for the construction of hotels on the same site. Photographs of some of the old inns and their modern replacements are included in this chapter.

Many other hotels too numerous to mention have been built, mostly on the Bath Road frontage of the airport. The major exception to this was the construction of the Post House Hotel (since re-named the Forte Crest Hotel) in the heart of the green belt between Harlington and Harmondsworth which, to the dismay of the local planning authority, was allowed on appeal in 1969. The inspector who conducted the inquiry recommended that the appeal should be allowed and stated in his report that the site, in the condition at that time, was 'at present of negligible visual interest and offered great opportunities for substantial landscaping which could be a major contribution to the M4 Linear Park. An hotel reaching to about 120 feet, set well back from the M4 would do no violence to any part of the M4 or its immediate surroundings,' [*sic*] (Report by V.L. Nash, FRIBA to Ministry of Housing and Local Government.)

To most people not trained as architects and not blessed with the breadth of vision of the inspector, the grotesque bulk of the hotel is, by any standards, a gross visual intrusion which dominates the skyline for miles around. For example, twenty-five years later, the Environmental Statement, prepared for the proposed widening of the M4 in the vicinity of the hotel, described the appearance of the hotel site as being 'largely negative in character with adverse effects on the locality'.

The Inspector's statement is a classic example of the double-standards which apply to the outcome of most planning appeals connected with Heathrow. Readers can judge for themselves, from the photograph, which of these two descriptions best represents the site.

The Post House Hotel, 1988. This has since been re-named the Forte Crest Hotel, of which it can be truly said 'I came, Eyesore, I conquered', and is a blot on the landscape for miles around. Gravel was extracted from what was formerly Grade 1 agricultural land in the foreground to provide material for the construction of the M4 motorway in 1963. It has remained derelict and unsightly ever since.

Milestone at Harlington Corner. The maintenance of the Bath Road in the vicinity of Heathrow was the responsibility of the Colnbrook Turnpike Trust. In 1741, as an aid to travellers, the Trust arranged to install stones at each mile of the road for which it was responsible. Many of these still remain, including this one at Harlington Corner.

The Coach and Horses and Ariel Hotel, Harlington Corner, 1961. A neat illustration of the change from the old and attractive to the new and ugly. The eighteenth-century coaching inn was a well-known local landmark but this did not save it when the Ariel (now the Post House) Hotel was built. As soon as the hotel was completed the inn was needlessly demolished. The hotel then attempted to reproduce an 'olde worlde' restaurant containing many spurious artefacts when it could so easily have retained the genuine article.

The Old Magpies, Bath Road, Heathrow, *c.* 1937. This sixteenth-century inn affectionately known locally as the Old Thatch stood on the south side of the Bath Road about 100 yards west of the similarly named Three Magpies (see below). In 1798 a Mr Mellish, brother of the MP for Grimsby was shot and robbed by two highwaymen outside the inn. He was taken into the 'Three Magpies' but died there before medical help arrived. A doctor summoned from Hounslow to give assistance was himself robbed by the same two men on his way to treat the injured man. It was needlessly demolished in 1951 and its site used for a car park until 1963 when the airport spur road was built through the area once occupied by the inn.

The Three Magpies, 1990. This public house dates from the eighteenth century. In 1765 it was known as the 'Three Pigeons' and later as the 'Magpie and Pigeon'. Although it has been extensively over-restored it is a unique survivor of the old coaching inns on the Bath Road near Heathrow. (See previous photograph on page 25.)

The Berkeley Arms, Bath Road, 1931 and 1998. The old Berkeley Arms stood on the north side of the Bath Road near to Cranford Bridge on the Harlington side. Like the Coach and Horses half a mile to the west, it was an eighteenth-century coaching inn serving the traffic on the Bath Road. It took its name from the Berkeley family who lived nearby at Cranford House until 1914. It was demolished when the Bath Road was widened in 1932 and the name transferred to a new public house, shown in the lower photograph, built in the style of a French château, about half a mile to the east at the junction of The Avenue with the Bath Road. This has since been extended and re-named the Jarvis International Hotel, although the armorial shield of the Berkeleys is still in place over the main entrance.

The Ostrich Inn, Colnbrook, 1998. Colnbrook, little more than two miles from the end of the main runway, was the lunch-time stop for stage-coaches out of London heading west and the final changing point for horses from the west to London. In airline parlance it was an important traffic hub and this is reflected in the many coaching inns which still line its High Street. The Ostrich, with its central carriageway to allow carriages into the yard behind, is unquestionably the finest of these. It dates from the twelfth century but the present building is largely early-sixteenth century.

Radisson Edwardian Hotel, 1998. This began life in the mid-1950s as the Skyways Hotel and was the first of the hotels to appear along the Bath Road frontage. It was built on the site of Bedford Lodge, a late-Georgian house which stood in a large garden. It was but the first example of the replacement of an old existing building in sympathy with its surroundings by modern system-built blocks of no architectural merit. The hotel was originally brick-faced and, although of no great distinction, it did not offend. In the 1980s it was re-modelled in a style best described as kitsch, with architectural features which would not look out of place in Las Vegas.

THE AIRPORT'S NEIGHBOURS

Surrounding the airport are what were once the old villages of West Middlesex – Cranford, Harlington, Sipson, Harmondsworth, Longford, Colnbrook, Poyle, Stanwellmoor, Stanwell, West Bedfont and East Bedfont. All are rich in history and architecture and struggle to survive and retain their identity. It is an uneven battle and some such as Cranford have already succumbed whilst others, such as Harmondsworth and Stanwell, still appear as oases in an urbanised desert beside a voracious neighbour which, if it has not yet managed to destroy them, casts a blight on the whole area around Heathrow.

In the case of Harlington, Sipson and Harmondsworth, a determined attempt has already been made to completely remove them from the map (see page 78). This threat was made again in the early 1990s and was only temporarily shelved. Few doubt that, if permission for the development of a fifth terminal were to be granted, BAA would seek once more to extend the airport to the north of the Bath Road.

The attitude of their insensitive neighbour is to regard the villages as mere adjuncts to the airport, exemplified by a BAA map which identified Harlington as 'Parking Zone 6'! If the residents have the temerity to complain, they are told that if they don't like the area they should move. The more affluent residents with no particular ties to the area, either by way of family or work, do of course move out, but 'tolerate or emigrate' is not an option for many people.

GETTING on with the neighbours is critical to the future development of the airport and its image. Tensions are bound to surface with the surrounding community wherever an operation exists on the scale of Heathrow, but Heathrow Airport Ltd (HAL) is keen to see these resolved.

Issues of concern to local residents include noise, congested roads, air quality and safety.

HAL is rightly concerned to ensure it always behaves as a good neighbour.

For over 20 years community links have been strengthened by the existence of Heathrow Airport Consultative Committee.

It was formed to provide an effective forum to 'thrash out' issues regarding the development and operation of Heathrow Airport which have an impact on people living and working in the surrounding areas.

The forum allows interested parties to be

Everybody needs good neighbours

The myth. BAA suffers from the delusion that it is environmentally responsible and a good neighbour of the local communities; the newspaper cutting shown above typifies its approach. Similarly, British Airways claims that its goal is 'to be a good neighbour concerned for the community and the environment!' Actions, quite literally in this case, speak louder than words. Good neighbours do not wake their fellow neighbours at 4.30 a.m., bombard them with noise all day and then threaten them with more noise when asked to be quieter.

The reality, or the neighbour from hell. Aircraft taking off over a house near the airport. Depending on wind direction and which runway is in use, overflying can occur for several hours at intervals of little more than two minutes. The only relief for those afflicted is when flights are switched to the other runway. If any employee of BAA inflicted a similar noise on his neighbours from his domestic activities or with his car he would be prosecuted, and imprisoned if he continued to be a nuisance. But citizens' rights to complain about aircraft noise are non-existent.

Village centres as off-airport car parks. In relation to the number of people arriving at Heathrow by car, there is only a limited amount of parking at the airport and what there is is very expensive to use. Strong pressures exist for off-airport parking on land around the airport, which is a very lucrative enterprise. Village centres, such as Harmondsworth, shown in the upper photograph, can become little more than gigantic car parks which are uncontrolled and completely ruin the appearance of what would otherwise be a pleasant area. The lower photograph shows a car park operating from the centre of Harlington. This particular parking site has planning permission, but many do not and unscrupulous owners can exploit loopholes in the planning regulations and operate with impunity for many years.

Church of St Peter & St Paul, Harlington. Harlington was first mentioned in an Anglo-Saxon land charter of AD 831 and again in the Domesday Survey of 1086. Its church dates from the twelfth century and has what is generally considered to be the finest Norman doorway in Middlesex. The village has suffered more than most from its proximity to the airport and most of its historic buildings have disappeared to make way for airport-related developments. Even the church came under threat when, in 1946, it was proposed to extend the airport up to the line of what is now the M4 motorway, and the threat remains.

Church of St Dunstan, Cranford. 'The church lies all on its own and is reached from the village by a drive and across a hump-backed bridge. There is great charm in this solitude.' So wrote Pevsner in the *Buildings of Middlesex* in 1951. Viewed from the south, as in this photograph, this still seems to be the case but it fails to reveal the presence of the M4 motorway only 100 yards to the north of the church. Nor can it reveal the deafening roar of traffic and aircraft in the once-peaceful churchyard.

Sipson House and Sipson Court, Sipson Road, Sipson. In 1969 this fine Grade II-listed Georgian house was still in good condition. Soon after, it became vacant and was purchased by BAA, after which it soon fell into the derelict condition shown in the photograph. Permission to 'restore' and convert it into offices was given in 1979, but the restoration involved total demolition except for the front façade. The new offices, re-named Sipson Court, are shown in the lower photograph. Although, apart from the side extensions, the building looks much the same, it is in fact a neo-Georgian replica and it is no longer a listed building because it has the same value to the real thing as does a mock antique to the genuine article. Many large houses of architectural interest in the vicinity of Heathrow have been converted to non-residential use in this way, but most have been genuine restorations rather than almost total reconstructions.

The Lodge, Harmondsworth Lane, *top*, 1974; *bottom*, 1984. This is another large house which has been converted to office accommodation, but in this case it was a genuine restoration. It was built in about 1800 and remained in residential use until the early 1960s when permission was given to convert the house into flats, but permission to develop the adjoining land to finance the conversion was refused. This left the house vacant and prey to vandalism and, as the upper photograph shows, the windows were boarded up and the house became ruinous. Eventually it was bought by APV International in 1977, who did a good job in restoring the interior to office accommodation. The lower photograph shows how well the original features of the house have been preserved.

Bath Road Farm and Heathrow Boulevard, Bath Road, Harmondsworth. At the time that the top photograph was taken in 1900, the Victorian (1866) farmhouse was the only building on the Bath Road between Longford and the Three Magpies. The author's great-grandfather Thomas Cottrell (1830–1909) stands outside his farmhouse with his daughter Emma. The name was later changed to Cedar Farm but became a private house when the farm lost most of its land to the Technicolor factory built in 1936. It later became derelict and was pulled down in 1969. The office block, Heathrow Boulevard, shown in the bottom photograph was built on the site of Bath Road Farm in the late 1980s. The change is characteristic of so much that has happened on the Bath Road between Longford and Harlington in recent years.

Harmondsworth Village. The village, which is less than half a mile from the airport's northern perimeter, still retains many of its old buildings. The oldest is the twelfth century church of St Mary which has a Norman doorway comparable with that of its neighbour at Harlington, a Tudor brick tower and a pretty cupola typical of the churches of West Middlesex. In the 1940s it was proposed that the village should be destroyed to make way for an extension of the airport. The threat was repeated again in the 1990s, with a proposed third runway for Heathrow occupying the site of the church.

The Great Barn of Harmondsworth. The Grade I-listed barn, which is also a scheduled ancient monument, stands just to the west of the church. It dates from about 1450 and, according to the late John Betjeman, is the finest medieval barn in England. It is certainly one of the largest, being 191 feet long and 38 feet wide and has survived virtually intact since it was first built. Although unique, it has been threatened more than once by demolition to make way for an extension of the airport.

Church of St Mary, East Bedfont. Bedfont parish was cut in half by the construction of the Great South West Road in the 1930s. Most of it to the north of the road, including much of the hamlet of Hatton, was then destroyed to make way for the airport. However, despite the proximity of the airport and the traffic, the central part around the village green and twelfth-century church still retains some semblance of a village character.

Stanwell Village. The village is hemmed in by the airport to the north and by reservoirs to the south-west which, paradoxically, help it to retain its own separate identity. The postcard shows (clockwise from top left-hand corner) Lord Knyvett's school (of 1624), the village fair, The Wheatsheaf and St Mary's Church.

Stanwell Village, 1993. Stanwell is the best-preserved of the airport villages and the top photograph, looking towards the twelfth-century church of St Mary, is deceptively rural. But the bottom photograph, taken from the top of the church tower and looking in the other direction, shows all too clearly the baleful influence of the airport.

Longford Village. Unlike its neighbours to the east, Longford at the western end of the northern runway, has never been threatened with physical destruction, but it suffers more than any other from the presence of the airport. If permission for a fifth terminal were to be granted, residents can expect up to twenty years of construction work on their doorsteps. The photograph shows the seventeenth-century White Horse in the centre of the village.

Colnbrook. The old Bath Road through Colnbrook is lined with several coaching inns (see page 97). The building in the foreground is known as King John's Palace and was once such an inn. It dates from the late sixteenth century; attached to it is the Star and Garter inn which was built some 100 years later.

CHAPTER ELEVEN

DEVELOPMENTS, 1960–90

THE FOURTH TERMINAL

Up to 1970 the only expansion of the airport, outside the boundaries set in 1952, was the extension of the northern runway to the west, approval for the construction of which was given in 1967. During the 1960s and early '70s it was becoming apparent that Heathrow and Gatwick, as they had been planned, would no longer be able to cope with the anticipated expansion of air traffic.

The cancellation in 1974 of the proposal to construct the third London Airport at Foulness (Maplin) increased pressure on Heathrow. Proposals were therefore made, in the mid-1970s, to expand the capacity of Heathrow by constructing a fourth terminal on the southern side of the airport outside its existing perimeter. The inspector's report of the public inquiry, the first ever to have been held over any development at Heathrow, was published in 1979. The result was, of course, a foregone conclusion: in his report the Inspector stated that 'in my view the present levels of noise around Heathrow are unacceptable in a civilised society', but this did not stop him from recommending that permission for the construction of a fourth terminal should be given. This decision in favour of the terminal was taken not because it was the preferred site, but because no other scheme of expansion could be carried out in time to meet the expected demand. The excuse given for the decision was 'overriding national necessity'. However, whilst recommending that approval for the expansion of the airport should be given, the inspector did go on to say:

> In the past the growth of Heathrow untrammelled by normal planning control has appeared to proceed without proper consideration for its effect on the environment especially in relation to noise. There is an inevitable danger that permission for T4 should be seen by some as yet another instance of precedence being given to the interests of travellers by air over the enjoyment of life by the local population. If this impression is to be dispelled it is, in my view, essential that if they decide to permit T4 the Secretaries of State should re-iterate that it is the Government's policy that there will be neither a fifth terminal nor any other major expansion of Heathrow.

The Government accepted these recommendations and it became official policy that once the fourth terminal was completed no further expansion would be permitted. This was made clear by a statement on 14 February 1980 when Lord Trefgarne, the then Government Aviation spokesman in the House of Lords, said: 'The Government conclude that the idea of a Fifth Terminal at Heathrow and a second runway at Gatwick should not be pursued. This effectively limits expansion at these airports.'

Construction of Terminal 4 went ahead and it opened to traffic in 1986. The lay-out of the airport after the terminal had been constructed is shown in the aerial photograph which appears on the next page.

Heathrow Airport from the air, *c.* 1990. Soon after the fourth terminal had been constructed on the south-eastern edge of the airport. It is remote from the three terminals in the central area and communication between the terminal and the centre is poor. On the western edge between the two main E–W runways is the Perry Oaks sludge works, the proposed site of the fifth terminal. Despite the assurances given at the T4 Inquiry even before the terminal opened, a determined attempt was made to obtain permission for a fifth terminal. (*Photograph courtesy of BAA plc*)

THE FIRST ATTEMPT AT A FIFTH TERMINAL, 1981

The Government's pledge not to expand Heathrow beyond a fourth terminal coupled with the growth in air traffic, increased the demand for a third London airport which had been shelved by the Maplin review. In the time-scale available it was decided that expansion of Stansted would be the optimum solution because it already had a suitable runway.

Proposals for the development of Stansted were submitted in July 1980, but the opponents of the proposal submitted an alternative planning application for the construction of a fifth terminal at Heathrow on the site of the Perry Oaks sludge works. This submission meant that the terms of reference of the inquiry into the expansion of Stansted had to be extended to include the possible construction of a fifth terminal at Heathrow.

The publicly-owned British Airports Authority (as it then was) was appalled by the counter-proposal and strongly argued against it. The December 1982 edition of its newsheet *Airport News* had the headline 'A Fifth Terminal – why BAA says no!' and a spokesman said: 'Most people assume that airports want to keep expanding regardless of the consequence to others. But as a responsible operator we want to do what is right for air passengers for the industry and the people who live near our airports [*sic*].'

The inspector's report of the Inquiry recommended that Stansted should be expanded and this recommendation was later accepted by the Government. In recommending the expansion of Stansted the inspector also recommended that: 'The applications made for planning permission for the extension of Heathrow Airport to provide a new passenger terminal complex and associated facilities and works on land at Heathrow Airport and Perry Oaks Sludge Disposal Works be refused.'

However, the Inspector gratuitously further recommended that 'Immediate Government and other action be taken to ensure that the Perry Oaks sludge treatment works is removed and that the site of the works, together with other necessary land to the west of the boundary with the M25, be taken into Heathrow Airport with the object of providing a fifth passenger terminal complex and other airport development with direct access to the motorway as soon as possible.'

This ensured that the possibility of further expansion of Heathrow was kept on the agenda; this despite the strong recommendation, endorsed by the Government at the T4 inquiry, that no such expansion should take place. Graham Eyre, the inspector at the T5 inquiry, had none of his predecessor's qualms and, in his report, he criticised the T4 inquiry inspector for making such a recommendation. He went to great lengths to make it clear that the only reason he had recommended that permission for the construction of a fifth terminal should be refused was because: 'It is unlikely that additional passenger terminal capacity could be constructed, commissioned and in operation at Heathrow in less than a decade from the date of decision to relocate Perry Oaks . . . Perry Oaks must be moved as expeditiously as possible, it must unquestionably go and its existence cannot reasonably be advanced as a reason for rejecting the expansion of Heathrow beyond four terminals.'

Much of the report of the first T5 inquiry reads like a eulogy for civil aviation and the Inspector recommended far more development than even aviation interests had asked for. However, few could disagree with his following statement:

The history and devlopment of airports policy on the part of administration after administration of whatever political colour has been characterised by ad hoc expediency, unacceptable and ill-judged procedures, ineptness, vacillation, uncertainty and ill-advised and precipitate judgements. Hopes of a wide sector of the regional population have been frequently raised and dashed. A strong public cynicism has inexorably grown. Political decisions in this field are no longer trusted. The consequences are grave. There will now never be a consensus. Other important policies which do not countenance substantial expansion of airport capacity or new airports have been allowed to develop and have become deeply entrenched. Somewhat paradoxically, such policies are heavily relied upon by thousands of reasonable people who strongly object to airport development. The past performance of Governments guarantees that any decision taken now will provoke criticism and resentment on a wide scale. I do not level this indictment merely as gratuitous criticism nor in order to fan the fires of the long history of controversy but to set the context for current decisions which will shape a future that must enjoy an appropriate measure of certainty and immutability.

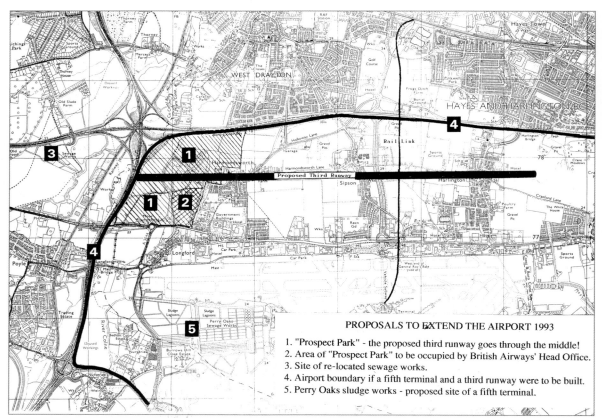

PROPOSALS TO EXTEND THE AIRPORT 1993

1. "Prospect Park" - the proposed third runway goes through the middle!
2. Area of "Prospect Park" to be occupied by British Airways' Head Office.
3. Site of re-located sewage works.
4. Airport boundary if a fifth terminal and a third runway were to be built.
5. Perry Oaks sludge works - proposed site of a fifth terminal.

Proposals to extend the airport, 1993. If all the plans came to fruition the airport boundary would be extended as far as the M4 motorway to the north and as far as the M25 motorway to the west. The plans for a fifth terminal, relocation of the Perry Oaks sludge works and the widening of the motorways, are the only positive proposals to date. However, once these were in place the other developments could quickly follow. (Reproduced from Pathfinder 1174 2½ in to 1 mile Ordnance Survey map by permission of the Controller of Her Majesty's Stationery Office © Crown Copyright MC88803M0001)

CHAPTER TWELVE

TOWARDS 2000 & BEYOND

The previous parts of the book have taken the history of Heathrow from prehistoric times up to 1990. This part considers the proposals for the future development of the airport into the twenty-first century. It is to be hoped that it will eventually be realised that we cannot go on extrapolating ever-rising forecasts of growth in air traffic indefinitely without suffering unacceptable environmental consequences. As a society we will need to pay a higher price for air travel to offset the unacceptable disturbance that is caused by the civil aviation industry. This fact has been recognised by the Royal Commission on Environmental Pollution which, in its report published in October 1994 on Transport and the Environment, stated: 'The demand for air transport might not be growing at the present rate if airlines and their customers had to face the costs of the damage they are causing to the environment.'

Development will inevitably come to a halt because, in the long term, the continued development of Heathrow will be impossible to sustain. There is, however, as yet little sign of any let-up in the pace of development. Quite the reverse, in fact, as the 1990s saw an increased pace in proposals for the further development of Heathrow on a far greater scale than anything seen in the first fifty years' growth of the airport.

The proponents of these various schemes were very careful to try to give the impression that they were not related, but they could be likened to a gigantic jigsaw and, as in the case of any jigsaw puzzle, each piece put into place would make it that much easier for the next piece to be inserted. If they all came about, the effect would be to double the area of land taken up by the airport with a consequent catastrophic increase in adverse environmental effects. The scenario included:

a) Finding an alternative site for the Perry Oaks sludge works.
b) Widening the motorway network around the airport so as to accommodate an increase in the expected number of passengers arriving at, and leaving, Heathrow by road.
c) The construction of a fifth terminal on the site of the Perry Oaks sludge works.
d) The construction by British Airways of a large office development for its Head Office on 5.3 hectares (13 acres) of green belt land north of the Bath Road (A4).

Concurrently with these proposals, a Committee was appointed by the Government to identify a site for an additional airport runway in the south-east. This Committee concluded that a third runway at Heathrow would be the best choice from the viewpoint of the aviation industry.

At the time of the first fifth-terminal inquiry, both the British Airports Authority and the Thames Water Authority were public utilities, ultimately answerable to the Government. Soon after the result of the inquiry was made known, both were privatised to become Public Limited Companies, known respectively as BAA plc and Thames Water plc. This action markedly changed the attitude of both bodies to the possibility of developing the site of the

Perry Oaks sludge works for a fifth terminal at Heathrow. While it was in public control, there was no real incentive for Thames Water to move from the Perry Oaks site. The land had been acquired very cheaply at pre-war agricultural prices and there would have been no advantage to the Thames Water Authority in 'selling' it for development as it would have gained no benefit from the sale. Nor would the Government have gained anything as the 'sale' would have been merely a paper transaction, with the value of the Perry Oaks site merely being transferred from one public utility (TWA) to another (BAA).

The privatisation of both authorities completely changed this position and gave every incentive to both BAA plc and Thames Water plc to find an alternative to Perry Oaks for its sludge disposal. As Heathrow is by far the most profitable of its airports, BAA, freed from Government policies that might run contrary to the expansion of the airport, was very keen to develop it to its maximum potential for the benefit of its shareholders. At the same time Thames Water would be in a position to gain a huge windfall profit if it could sell the land to BAA.

However, construction of a fifth terminal could not even begin before the Perry Oaks sludge works had been closed down, and this could not be done until a solution had been found for the disposal of the sludge from Mogden, which clearly had to go somewhere. Thames Water therefore began an investigation to find an alternative method for de-watering the sludge from Mogden which would require less space than the method originally used at Perry Oaks. The solution to the problem was to de-water the sludge by mechanical means to produce a final product with a dry-solids content of about 25 per cent. This could be stacked within storage areas on site using a mechanical conveyor system, whence it would be taken away and used on farmland in the same way as the sludge already being produced by the works at Perry Oaks. The mechanical de-watering of the sludge was put into effect at Perry Oaks in the mid-1990s, which released 90 per cent of the Perry Oaks site for other development and made it easier to transfer the operation to another site if, and when, the need arose.

Spelthorne Farm, 1994. This rural scene adjoins the Perry Oaks sludge works and is only 200 yards from the end of the southern runway. It is destined to become part of the fifth terminal complex.

Top: Perry Oaks sludge works. Bottom: Iver South Sewage Works, 1994. The top photograph shows the sludge works at Perry Oaks with the Duke of Northumberland's River, which comes up for air at Perry Oaks. The proposed site for the transfer of the sludge works is the Iver South sewage works seen in the lower photograph. This lies to the south of the M4 between Junction 4b (with the M25) and Junction 5 (with the A4 at Langley), some two miles to the north-west of Perry Oaks. (The name of the works is misleading because it is a considerable distance from Iver and is much nearer to Colnbrook on the south side of the M4.) The existing sewage works at Iver South is already owned by Thames Water and occupies 15.5 acres. It is anticipated that an additional nine acres would be required for the proposed development – a total of 24.4 acres, less than one-tenth of the area occupied by the Perry Oaks works.

Site on Harmondsworth Moor for British Airways' Corporate Business Centre. The site is just to the north of the Colnbrook bypass and is bounded on the east by the Duke of Northumberland's River and on the west by the River Colne. For this reason it has been named 'Waterside' by British Airways. The top photograph shows the site as it appeared in 1992 before any development and the bottom photograph shows the site from the same vantage point just before the complex was opened in 1998. In return for receiving planning permission for the development, BA agreed to landscape the surrounding area of Harmondsworth Moor and lay it out as a public park. If the proposed third runway at Heathrow were ever to be built it would go through this park (see map on page 112). The site of the BA offices would then be well-placed to become the sixth terminal.

EFFECTS OF A THIRD RUNWAY
(RUCATSE Report 1993)

Demolitions:

Houses	3,300
Listed buildings	44
Public Buildings	11
Hotels	10
Other commercial	15,000
(m² floorspace)	

Landtake for enlargement (hectares):

Area of existing airport	1,197
Area of enlarged airport	1,862
Total landtake	665
Green Belt	602
of which:	
Grade 1 Land	427
Other agricultural	22
Recreational	59

Additional landtake for relocations: 1,500 ha. (6 square miles)

Acquisition/relocation costs	**£1,162 m (1992 prices)**
Total construction costs	**£3,271 m**

In 1990 the Department of Transport set up a Working Group on Runway Capacity to Serve the South-East (RUCATSE). The Committee acknowledged that, apart from the demolitions that were envisaged, the extra noise generated by a third runway at Heathrow would disturb ten times as many people as any of the other options and double the number of people already adversely affected by noise from Heathrow. However, this did not deter it from the further pursuit of Heathrow as a strong contender for the construction of an additional runway and in its final report it recommended Heathrow as being the preferred option for an additional runway in the south-east.

The Government rejected the RUCATSE recommendation for Heathrow while acknowledging that a site for a third runway would have to be found somewhere in the south-east. Which raises the question: if not Heathrow, where else should it go? It is widely suspected that, if and when it gained permission for a fifth terminal, BAA would be back for more, as it and its predecessors have done so often on previous occasions.

Sipson Lane, Harlington, 1995. The route of Sipson Lane roughly follows the line of the middle section of the proposed third main runway at Heathrow. The view is from the Harlington end looking westwards towards Sipson. The houses on the right are Westfield Cottages.

Church and the Great Barn, Harmondsworth, 1998. This view was taken from the banks of the Duke of Northumberland's River and although very recent, it could have been taken at any time in the last 150 years. It was referred to in Pevsner's *Buildings of England* as an 'all too rare glimpse of the quiet, uneventful Middlesex countryside, with barn and church rising above the willow-lined water meadows'. If a third runway at Heathrow were ever to be built, and it has been seriously considered, it would go through the middle of this picture.

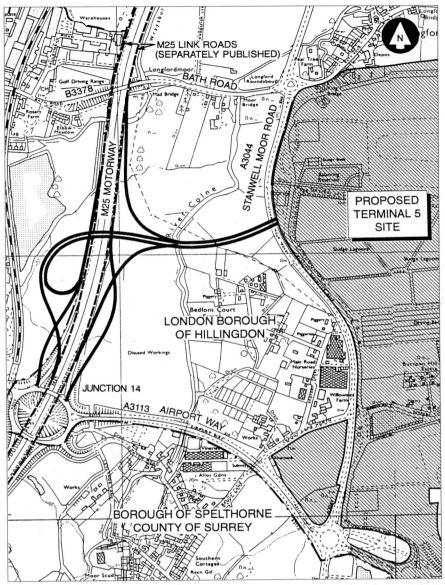

Road access to Heathrow. The major motorway link for Heathrow is the M25 which was built to link together the other motorways around London. It had been started in 1975 and the final section of its 120 miles was formally opened by Margaret Thatcher on 29 October 1986. By then it was already becoming a national joke or a disgrace, depending on whether or not one used it. Although Margaret Thatcher, notorious for lacking any sense either of humour or of proportion, did not see it that way. She boldly declared: 'Some people are saying that the road is too small. Even that it is a disaster. I must say that I cannot stand those who carp and criticise when they ought to be congratulating Britain on a magnificent achievement.' Although it was denied by BAA and the Department of Transport, there was obviously a link between the proposals to widen the M25 and to construct a fifth terminal at Heathrow. This is clear from the fact that when BAA submitted its planning application, it included the construction of a spur road to link the terminal directly to a widened M25. This would be the only road link between the terminal and the motorway network.

Traffic jam on the M4 – Airport Spur Road, 1994. Because of such problems it is proposed to widen this road to four lanes in each direction, but not to widen the two-lane tunnel into which it leads!

Anti-road propaganda. The proposals to widen the M25 and M4 motorways were fiercely resisted and the original plans for a 14-lane M25 had to be completely abandoned. The plans were scaled down further on several subsequent occasions but even the final plans met with strong opposition.

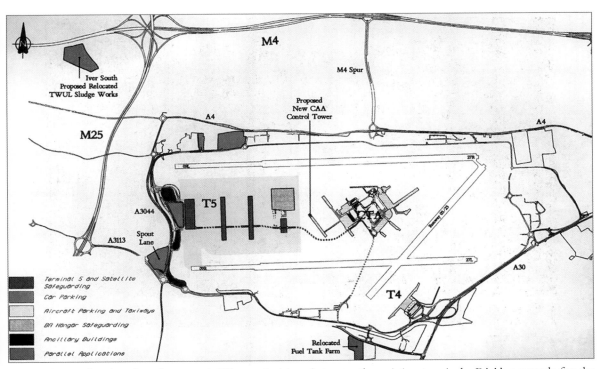

Airport layout showing site of proposed fifth terminal in relation to the existing terminals. BAA's proposals for the construction of a fifth terminal at Heathrow on the Perry Oaks site were first put forward in 1992. The proposed terminal was to consist of a core building, three satellites, aircraft stands, aprons and taxiways, car parks, ancillary buildings and a hotel site. These developments would be on such a scale as to make the complex bigger than the existing four terminals put together. The proposals and the associated developments represented the biggest single project in south-east England in the last fifty years. Such a massive development obviously had to be the subject of a public inquiry and, apart from the proposed construction of a fifth terminal, the Government announced that the Inquiry would also consider the associated developments of the removal of the sludge works from Perry Oaks to Iver South, the construction of a spur road to link the terminal to the M25, and the widening of the M4 and M25 in the vicinity of the airport.

Dear Neighbour

Our parent company, BAA plc, has put forward proposals for a fifth terminal at Heathrow – a world-class development to meet the needs and quality standards of people wanting to fly in the 21st century.

Over the next few months, we'll be consulting extensively with the local authorities before we finalise our planning application. Meanwhile, we've prepared this leaflet to keep you informed about our ideas so far. I hope you'll find time to read it and form your own conclusions.

No airport can be invisible and inaudible. But we aim to live in harmony with our neighbours, and the proposals for Terminal 5 will be designed to minimise its impact on local communities. *In particular, I'd like to reassure you that they will NOT require another runway or an increase in night flights. You'll find more details about this on page 6.*

We believe the proposals balance the interests of neighbours, passengers, employees and our business. When you've read this leaflet, I hope you'll support us in our efforts to keep Heathrow the world's number one international airport, with its consequent benefits to the local and national economies.

As our plans and consultations develop, I'll make sure we keep you up to date. If you want to know more in the meantime, we've set up a special Terminal 5 telephone information line – full details are on page 8. Our information team will do their best to answer any questions you may have.

Mike Roberts

Mike Roberts
Managing Director
Heathrow Airport Limited

BAA propaganda in favour of T5. Front page of leaflet headed 'Dear Neighbour' setting out reasons behind BAA's proposals for a fifth terminal. BAA claimed that the huge increase in the proposed capacity of the airport (from 50 million to 80 million passengers per year) would not lead to a demand for a third runway nor to a demand for an increase in the number of night flights, nor to a rise in noise levels. Among the reasons it gave was that the key to handling such a large growth in passengers, without a proportionate increase in flights, was the increased use of wide-bodied jets in modern airline fleets. It anticipated the introduction of even bigger jets, seating up to 800 people, and claimed that without Terminal 5 the airport would not be able to handle as many of these huge aircraft as the airlines might want to use. These jets do not, as yet, exist and it is by no means certain that they ever will as Boeing, the world's largest aircraft manufacturer, has abandoned its plans for a superjumbo jet. Speaking at a conference on air transport held by the Institute of Economic Affairs in London in December 1998, the Chief Executive of British Airways was quoted as saying: 'The industry had changed direction and that jets were getting smaller. Passengers wanted greater flight frequency and it was more efficient for airlines to fly more often with smaller aircraft than once a day with giant jets'. A consequent increase in the number of smaller jets using T5 would inevitably lead to rising demands for a third runway.

Local authority opposition to a fifth terminal. The inquiry proved to be the most formidable opposition that BAA had ever had to face and its first as a private company rather than as an arm of the Government. Most of the local authorities around the airport were opposed to the further expansion of Heathrow and ten of these combined together to form a consortium – Local Authorities Against Heathrow's T5 (LAHT5) – to pay the costs of making representations at the inquiry. Hillingdon Council, within whose boundaries most of the airport lies, not only decided to oppose the development, but also paid the costs of separate representation at the Inquiry. Thus BAA unexpectedly found itself up against not one but two formidable opponents (Hillingdon and LAHT5), which in the legal power they could jointly mobilise were – for once – the equals of BAA and British Airways.

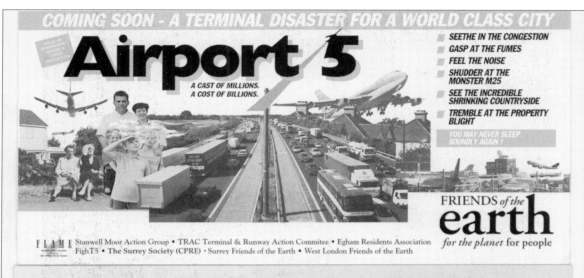

COMING SOON - A TERMINAL DISASTER FOR A WORLD CLASS CITY

Airport 5

A CAST OF MILLIONS.
A COST OF BILLIONS.

- SEETHE IN THE CONGESTION
- GASP AT THE FUMES
- FEEL THE NOISE
- SHUDDER AT THE MONSTER M25
- SEE THE INCREDIBLE SHRINKING COUNTRYSIDE
- TREMBLE AT THE PROPERTY BLIGHT

YOU MAY NEVER SLEEP SOUNDLY AGAIN !

FRIENDS *of the* **earth**
for the planet for people

FLAME Stanwell Moor Action Group • TRAC Terminal & Runway Action Commitee • Egham Residents Association
FighT5 • The Surrey Society (CPRE) • Surrey Friends of the Earth • West London Friends of the Earth

T5 - National Issue, Local Concern, Test of Government

Heathrow Terminal 5 is a national issue. What happens at Heathrow will dictate airport and air travel policy across the UK, Europe and beyond. T5 is a test of the Labour Government's commitment to an integrated transport system and:

- people's health
- a mixed economy
- the planning system
- green belt policy
- environmental quality
- action on climate change

When you see BAA's expensive presentations and gimmicky gifts (got the T5 pen and badge set yet?) consider:

ECONOMY - T5 has nothing to do with people's real need to fly or with benefits to the UK economy. It's really about profits for BAA who before privatisation said T5 was not needed.

EMPLOYMENT - In the media BAA say T5 will boost employment but at the T5 inquiry they admit T5 will have minimal effect on jobs.

COMPETITION - BAA refuse to say how much expansion is enough. Is T5 just the start of never ending expansion with 'competition' with European airports used as an easy excuse? Does Britain's status really depend on a single development?

PROFITS - Why is T5 mostly a shopping mall (almost four times the size of Wembley Stadium) on supposedly protected Green Belt land? CLUE: BAA's most profitable business is retailing.

INTEGRATED TRANSPORT - BAA are so committed to public transport that: 1.T5 will increase parking at Heathrow to 46,000 spaces. 2.BAA's much trumpeted plans for public transport are not part of the planning application.

NATIONAL ROADS NETWORK - Why is T5 so dependent on a widened M25? Is the public purse about to pay for the benefit of a private company?

AIRPORTS POLICY - BAA say T5 will not lead to a third runway at Heathrow If that's true, why are BAA lobbying Mr Prescott for more runways in the South East?

NATIONAL POLICY - Is Mr Prescott going to allow BAA and its friends (British Airways) to dictate national transport policy?

YOU CAN'T TRUST BAA - They can't even get their figures right. Example: telling the Inquiry that predicted flights without T5 will reach 420,000 by 2016 when by 1995 they had already reached 415,000.

'T5/ M 25 Enough is Enough, Mr Prescott'

JUST SOME OF THE NATIONAL ISSUES - MORE?   CONTACT US - 0171 566 1678

Environmental protest groups' propaganda against T5. Apart from the local authorities around Heathrow, opposed to the development, many environmental groups and residents' associations also registered as objectors and appeared at the inquiry to give evidence and cross-examine BAA and its allies. The progress of the T5 development had already slipped by one year by the time that the first pre-inquiry meeting was held in May 1994. At that meeting the inspector stated that he anticipated that the main inquiry would start in May 1995 and that it would go on for at least eighteen months (i.e. until late 1996). This proved to be wildly optimistic as the unexpectedly large number of organisations opposed to BAA, the degree of expertise on which they could draw, and the incredible commitment of some of the environmental groups, meant that the Inquiry lasted far longer than anticipated. BAA had assumed that the Inquiry would begin in 1994 and end in 1995 and in the normal course of events this would not have been an unreasonable assumption. At most public inquiries a developer faces only one major antagonist, but for each topic of the T5 Inquiry BAA never faced fewer than four. The large number of people presenting evidence and the time taken up in cross-examination was not foreseen even by BAA's opponents and in the event the inquiry lasted until March 1999. BAA had proposed that the fifth terminal should be built in stages. It hoped that the first phase would open in 2002 and that it would provide for ten million passengers a year. The final phase, which BAA hoped would be completed by 2016, would bring the total capacity of the terminal to thirty million passengers a year. Instead, because of the strength and ferocity of the opposing groups, the inquiry lasted nearly four years – the longest ever. The earliest date for construction to begin, even if approval is given, is now (in 1999) 2003.

Demonstrators against the T5 development. Above, at the opening of the Inquiry on 16 May 1995 and below, at the second anniversary in 1997. Around 22,000 individuals and organisations sent written representations to the Inquiry Secretariat, of which 96 per cent were opposed to the development. The opposition was also reflected in the local public sessions of the inquiry, at which members of the public were given the chance to express their views. At these sessions 290 people came forward of whom 243 (84 per cent) spoke against T5. The crude home-made banners of the protest groups which can be seen in the photographs were in stark contrast to the glossy propaganda of BAA. However, what these groups lacked in funds they made up in commitment.

BAA barrister, Guy Roots QC, said: "Even if it was to be concluded that the development would cause demonstrable harm in terms of air quality, that conclusion would have to be weighed against other material considerations in order to reach a decision as to whether or not planning permission should be granted for T5."

"NO, DEAR, THEY'RE NOT ASTRONAUTS — THEY JUST WORK AT HEATHROW AIRPORT."

Cartoon mocking BAA's attitude to air pollution. Concern was expressed at the T5 Inquiry about the effects of air pollution from the airport on the health of those who live in its vicinity. This provoked the extraordinary response from counsel for BAA that is lampooned in the cartoon which appeared in the *Hayes Gazette* in April 1998.

Apart from the health effects of air pollution it is claimed that carbon dioxide from air traffic over Europe is increasing the greenhouse effect as much as cars, power stations and shipping combined. Because of such concerns, in 1994 the Royal Commission on Environmental Pollution considered that: 'There is a powerful case on environmental grounds for regulatory action to avert what could be irreversible damage to the earth's atmosphere from the growth of air traffic, or at least serious damage of a long-term nature.'

A gravel pit near Heathrow. Material from this pit, on Grade 1 agricultural land, was used in the construction of the fourth terminal. A fifth terminal would lead to increased demand for aggregate, with damaging effects, such as this, well outside the Heathrow area. The fifth terminal, taken in conjunction with the associated road and other developments, makes it the biggest single civil engineering project to be proposed in south-east England in the last fifty years. Huge amounts of aggregates would be required for the T5 development. Merely to cover the Perry Oaks site with 1 metre of hardstanding would require about 2½ million tonnes of aggregate. The total amount of aggregates required could well amount to half of the annual production of aggregate within the south-east.

BIBLIOGRAPHY

Balfour, H.H., *Wings over Westminster* London, Hutchinson, 1973

BAA, Heathrow. *Heathrow Airport – Facts and Figures*, 3rd edn. 1997

Bennett, L.G., *The Horticultural Industry of Middlesex*, Department of Agricultural Economics, University of Reading, 1952

Buchanan, C., *No Way to the Airport* London, Longmans, 1981

Cotton, J., Mills J. and Clegg, G., *Archaeology in West Middlesex*, Hillingdon Borough Libraries, 1986

Department of the Environment, *Sustainable Development: The UK Strategy* Cm.2426, London, HMSO, 1994

Eyre, Graham, *The Airports Inquiries 1981–1983* (Expansion of Stansted: Fifth Terminal at Heathrow), Report in nine volumes – no date or publisher given

Glidewell, I.D.L., Report of the fourth terminal inquiry, London, HMSO, 1979

Grimes, W.F. A., 'Prehistoric temple at London Airport', *Archaeology*, 1948, 1 (1), 74–78

Hall, Peter, *Great Planning Disasters*, London, Weidenfeld & Nicolson, 1983

Hayter, George, *Heathrow – The Story of the World's Greatest International Airport*, London, Pan Books, 1989

Highways Agency (Department of Transport), *Heathrow Terminal 5 Access, M25 Spur Road and M4 Junctions 3 to 4B* Environmental Statement 1994

Masefield, Peter, 'Heathrow Airport – Past, Present and Future', Fourteenth Fairey Memorial Lecture to Royal Aeronautical Society (Heathrow Branch), 19 October 1972 (unpublished)

Maxwell, G., *Highwayman's Heath*, Hounslow, Thomasons, 1935

Norris, P. The History of Aviation at Heston, *From Airships to Concorde: A History of Aviation in West London*, Chiltern Aviation Society (undated)

Public Record Office, Files listed principally under AIR 19, AVIA 2 and BT 217

Rowlands, P., 'The Duke of Northumberland's River', *The Honeslaw Chronicle*, 2, Hounslow History Society, 1987

Roy, W., 'Account of the measurement of a base on Hounslow Heath', *Royal Society Philosophical Transactions* LXXV (1785)

Royal Commission on Environmental Pollution, Eighteenth Report: *Transport and the Environment*, London, HMSO, 1994

RUCATSE: Runway Capacity to Serve the South East, A Report by the Working Group, Department of Transport, July 1993

Sherwood, P.T., *Agriculture in Harmondsworth Parish – Its Growth and Decline 1800–1970*, West Drayton Local History Society, 1973

——. *The History of Heathrow*, Hillingdon Library Services, 1990

Stamp, L. Dudley, 'Land Classification and Agriculture' *Greater London Development Plan, 1944* London, HMSO, 1944

Willatts, E.C., *Middlesex and the London Region*, Report of the Land Utilisation Survey No. 79, 1937

ACKNOWLEDGEMENTS

Acknowledgements to commercial organisations for reproducing their photographs are given, where appropriate, in the text. Particular thanks are due to Graham Smeed who provided several photographs from his private collection and prepared good quality prints from some of the author's poor quality originals. In addition, the author would like to thank the West Drayton and District Local History Society, HACAN, West London FOE, Ms A. Glenie, Mrs R. McManus, Ms J. Shane, F.J. Chinery, S.J. Heyward, J. Marshall, K.R. Pearce, K. Ratling, D.M. Rust, P. Russell, B.T. White, and W.L. Wild for the provision of several illustrations used in the book. The maps on pages 62, 76 and 78 are based on Crown copyright material in the Public Record Office and are reproduced by permission of the Controller of Her Majesty's Stationery Office.

INDEX